Graham Cooke

Coming into Alignment

An Interactive Journal

WAY OF THE WARRIOR Series ... 3

Brilliant Book House LLC
6391 Leisure Town Road
Vacaville, California 95687
U.S.A.
www.BrilliantBookHouse.com

Unless otherwise indicated, all Scripture quotations are taken from The Holy Bible, New King James Version (Copyright © 1979, 1980, 1982 by Thomas Nelson, Inc.) and the New American Standard Bible (Copyright © 1960, 1962, 1963, 1972, 1973, 1975, 1977, 1995 by The Lockman Foundation).

Requests   for   information   should   be   addressed   to:
Office@GrahamCooke.com

ISBN 978-1-934771-10-5

Special Edition printed by Integrity Media Europe with permission.
Integrity Media Europe
Unit 1, Hargreaves Business Park
Hargreaves Road,
Eastbourne, BN23 6QW U.K.

Endorsements

In this book, Graham Cooke focuses on the key issues of bringing heaven to earth. He emphasizes the need for a new sight of Christ which produces a clarified sense of identity. He rejects natural reason and rationalism in favor of the mind of Christ that has a realization of the unseen realm where the core of real action lies. Graham focuses on authentic connection to God which produces the ability to overcome. In being aligned with the values of the Kingdom of God we become like the One who overcomes all things. This book is a valuable resource not only because of what Graham presents, but also how he presents it. Graham is a father and a guide that leads the reader through a correct process of development and maturity towards the ultimate destination of Christ likeness.

Scott Webster
World Breakthrough Network

I have loved the Way of the Warrior series including Qualities of a Spiritual Warrior and Manifesting Your Spirit. I have been doing these with a group of warrior men each Friday morning. Our lives are changing and being transformed. Coming into Alignment is another brilliant book by

Graham. I love the part on the two routes into alignment---impartation and process and what they do in our lives. If you want to be a warrior for the Lord or you are a warrior for the Lord this is a cutting edge book. It is very practical and heart changing. My wife, Terry and I love you Graham and Theresa and all you deposit into us. Thank you.

Dan Hammer
Sonrise Chapel Senior Pastor
Northwest New Wine Network, WA

"We learn about the nature of God because He applies His heart to ours." Wow! Great line! Graham is so gifted at simplifying deep truths; his writings impart to us the profound wonder of God's extravagant love. An amazing read. Hope-filled. Yes, whatever the assignment I receive. Yes, I align my heart, my all. And yes, may I be *"too busy being fascinated by Jesus."*

Karen Padgett
Director of Retail Sales
John Fluevog Shoes

Graham reveals again his spiritual authority as a father/leader to Kingdom-minded Christians.

"Coming into Alignment" is a training regiment for the special forces type warriors of the Kingdom.

Here, yet again, Graham is consistent in his faithfulness to press into the heart of majesty where he hears the edicts of the King regarding warfare and strategies against the enemy.

In this series of books, Graham speaks with bold authority and a father's love, appealing to the body of Christ to embrace maturing with the intentionality these times demand. It is an invitation with empowerment, offering to move us past all redundant desires to remedy our circumstances, and bring to an end the joy-impoverished exhaustion that comes with a conserving mindset of measure—into our inherent right of being joy-filled weapons of abundance.

Michael Galeotti
Founder Wild Branch Christian Ministries
Former Marine

Graham has an ever increasing capacity to shine light into spiritual matters so that your heart glows with desire for God. COMING INTO ALIGNMENT powerfully penetrates the mis-understanding of who God is for us and what we can accomplish for His kingdom. Your life with God will enter extraordinary places as the revelation Graham has received settles in your heart. Your life in the Spirit is going to access the dimensions promised in God's word.

Peter McHugh
Pastor, C3 Centre
Melbourne, Australia

Coming into Alignment provides an essential, balanced and proper understanding of every believer's place in God and in spiritual warfare. *Coming into Alignment* encourages and helps readers experience the truths in this book, not just read them. These truth encounters create perspective and paradigm. While reading some of these chapters, I realized once again that so many of the thoughts I currently consider "my own" are a result of years of being mentored and aligned by Graham's visits, talks and writings. As a refresher or a revelation, the insights here are "spot on" for the times we live in today.

David Danielson
Pastor, Impact Christian Fellowship
Kerrville, TX

Coming into Alignment drew me into a fresh discovery of the divine adventure and privileged lifestyle we can enjoy as Kingdom Warriors. Graham describes a way of life that draws us into a daily, living, face-to-Face relationship with God. He inspires us to discover what awaits us in this place of intimacy: personal transformation, greater authority, and a new level of overcoming power. As always, I love the way Graham makes the profound practical, as he leads us on a journey into the wonder and power of His Majesty.

Dena McClure Ministries
The Mission
Vacaville, CA

Dedication

I dedicate this book to a great friend and fellow warrior, Jane Hansen-Hoyt, President of Aglow International and to all her compatriots in arms at H.Q. and the tens of thousands that she commands around the world, both men and women. I dedicate this book especially to the women of Aglow, people who have been around for years and have faithfully served, women who by their dedication and commitment have interceded for the church and the Kingdom. Without them we would not have gotten this far.

Aglow is an elite company of warriors, champions, commanders, special forces, and spiritual marines. Women are great fighters - tireless, dedicated, and consistent. There is an ancient curse upon the enemy that he will always be beaten by a woman and by what she produces [Genesis 3:14-15]. The enemy may bruise her heel, but she will crush his head. Actually, I think it is more that she will so violently stamp on him that her foot will become sore.

No wonder then the violence that is perpetrated on women all around the globe. My association with Aglow has been of huge benefit to me. When you stand in front of these women you need to be moving in something majestic, because they will call it up in you!

They are passionate in their pursuit of intimacy with the Lord and ferocious in their battle against the enemy. There is a good reason why they are called girrrrls!!

Acknowledgements

Firstly, to Pam Jarvis my international prayer coordinator, personal friend, and commander of a growing number of prayer partners across the world who pray for my ministry.

Pam has a fabulous group of coordinators who lead hundreds of partners in prayer that covers every aspect of the ministry. I am amazed at Pam's indefatigable nature. She brings an energetic zeal to all she does. Her co-conspirators who help her coordinate the different regions and nations around the world are all highly motivated and powerful. They organize my shield wall and support me magnificently in the ongoing battle against darkness. We're winning!

Also to Jeanne Thompson who has moved on to other things but thankfully is still staying in Vacaville. We miss her, talk about her, and love her. My thanks for all her hard work and dedication.

Finally, allow me to introduce Jenny Percey, my new personal assistant. She began in September, and we are amazed at how well she has settled in and made the role hers. She is a quick study, an excellent worker, who will become a key member of the team. She is funny, a delight, and has captured all our hearts effortlessly.

Contents
Coming into Alignment

Alignment is Majestic

"*He that is in you is greater than he that is in the world [1 John 4:4] because "whatever is born of God overcomes the world." [1 John 5:4]. As He is so are we in this world." [1 John 4:17]*

If alignment does not focus on magnificence it is not worth anything. We are lining up with Jesus, in Jesus, and behind Jesus. Therefore, before we can add to our own identity we must first fully understand His. Secondly, we must embrace and fully experience the power of His identity in our own lives.

If we are to become aligned in all respects to Jesus we must move beyond measure to fullness. The life of Jesus contains every last ounce of the fullness of God physically. As He indwells us, that same fullness makes us complete and provokes us into a place of authority and rule over the enemy [Colossians 2:9-10].

It is part of our journey that our heart becomes thoroughly cognizant of the incredible life that the Father has bestowed upon us in Christ. We are His inheritance in the earth, and He is ours. Unless we see and experience that inheritance, we can never possess it to the same level of power that the Father desires.

There is strength in alignment that brushes aside the enemy and reveals the fullness of power in

Christ. Alignment is for the high places in God. It guarantees that we can stay in the rarefied atmosphere of abundance - to the point where our expectation of God is so strong, the enemy will back off from a fight.

Alignment is atmospheric. It lifts us up to the place of majesty. The eyes of our heart are illuminated. We see all that He sees, and we are swallowed up in majesty. We understand what it fully means to be the church as we experience God's magnificence. We are no longer coming from behind in our battle with the enemy. Majesty introduces us to the power of constant subjection. Alignment creates a new place of authority, one that is attached to the fullness of Jesus. Our inheritance springs forth from that place as we taste the power of this age and the one to come. Surpassing greatness becomes the norm for a spiritual warrior whose heart is set on alignment [Ephesians 1:18-23].

Fullness relates to all that God is and wants to be in each of us. It is spirituality so rare and generous that it sets us apart from the usual. Only fullness can truly glorify God. Only majesty can perfectly reveal His nature.

We need a clear, visual definition of His total supremacy. It is our point of origin where we find ourselves, adapting to the prevailing level of light - able to see clearly and to know majesty by experience. We are lost in the wonder of God's splendor, absorbed

13

by the King, elevated by glory. His majesty becomes our fixed point; His radiant nature the center of our attraction.

In that place of alignment, love conquers us fully. Every part of our being is touched and infiltrated. We become engrossed with the beauty of God's nature. We are taken up into a high place, stranded on a mountain top as the glory of His goodness parades before us, and we hear the joyous proclamation of God's nature from His own lips.

The glory of alignment is that we can understand all that God is to us. Every part of our heart and mind is expanded in a way that is compatible with abundance [Ephesians 3:16-20].

Measure limits us severely. It diminishes our thinking, believing, and experience. It corrupts our prayer to childish gibberish. Abundance makes us fully mature in childlike exclamations of glory. Abundance and exuberance go together. They empower us into a place of maturity where the stature of the fullness of Christ is revealed [Ephesians 4:13].

Before the Cross, Jesus shows us what is possible for a righteous man to be and do before God. He is God's visual aid to thoroughly enlighten humanity. After the Cross, His indwelling presence brings a reality of Heaven into our hearts. As it is in heaven, so it can be on earth; this is the Lord's prayer for us.

Spiritual warriors have learned to resist the enemy and overcome the circumstances facing them. They know how to release heaven by speaking peace and blessing over everything and everyone around them. They have developed an ability to contribute positively to the spiritual atmosphere.

The enemy is the prince of the power of the air [Ephesians 2:2]; he lives in the atmosphere. Spiritual warriors are perceptive. When they encounter a wrong atmosphere something rises up within them, and they have to check it out.

Walking through a mall in Southern England, I hit this brick wall in the spirit. One moment I was enjoying the Lord; the next, I was assailed by a sense of hopelessness. I backtracked a few yards and recovered myself. Repositioning is one of the attributes of alignment.

When I was ready I walked forward again in the permission of the Holy Spirit. I saw a long line of people waiting and then discovered a psychic booth. This man was reading palms, telling fortunes, reaching the dead, and doing tarot cards. According to the sign, he was there every Tuesday and Thursday.

Partnering with the Holy Spirit is another attribute of alignment. It is a partnership that is relentless against the enemy. I began to walk around the booth quietly speaking in tongues and worshipping majesty. We don't have to be loud or draw attention to ourselves. Our joy is to penetrate the atmosphere and burst the enemy's balloon. It is better to do it under the radar. I watched as this man turned from being animated, excited, and commanding attention to a place of confusion and being flustered. Eventually he stopped. "The vibrations have left," he said as he packed up his gear. I made sure for the next few weeks that each Tuesday and Thursday afternoon, there were no vibrations in that mall. He never returned.

Spiritual warriors are constantly on assignment towards the enemy because they are aligned with majesty. We do not go looking for the enemy unless we have specific permission from the Holy Spirit. It is rather that whenever we encounter him in life we have the freedom to move in our alignment. That means that we are not touched by what he is doing because the manifest Presence of Jesus occupies our inner space.

Warriors are subject to wisdom especially when it comes to warfare strategy and tactics. We automatically know when our internal power can overcome the atmosphere. In the same way we know when it is prudent to step back and listen to the Holy Spirit. Some situations require more warriors.

It is one of the reasons why I have over 400 intercessors praying for my ministry. Some of them are powerful warriors in the Spirit who give me much needed spiritual intelligence about the location I am to travel into as well as the breakthroughs that I can expect to see under the anointing.

For me this has meant the difference between accepting an invitation from people to actually taking an assignment from the Lord.

We first push the enemy back in our own inner space. Jesus said, "The prince of this world has come but he has nothing on me" [John 14:30]. Alignment maintains a clean and pure heart. From this place of freedom we can dispense freedom. "It is for freedom that Christ has set us free." [Galatians 5:1].

It is vital then that we are overwhelmed by the freedom of the Lord: that we revel in majesty and become preoccupied with His greatness. As the Holy Spirit enables our hearts to define the majesty of God, so He will move us into the correct position before His throne. When we come to prayer in that place, our intercession is not concerned with the power of the enemy, but is focused instead on the ascendancy of the Lord Jesus.

We begin to determine what it feels like to have an ascended lifestyle in Jesus. We pray from a place of rest, seated with Christ in heavenly places far above earthly dominions. The power of constant subjection is realized through the authority of the Lord Jesus.

Warriors must deal with majesty. The fullness of the splendor of Christ must take root in our hearts and produce fruit in our minds. When our believing and our thinking are fully engaged in majesty, we will rise up effortlessly and occupy the place of our inheritance, which the Father has set aside for us.

Assignment

❋ What will it take for you to believe that God is unceasingly magnificent towards you?
❋ Journal that through in the space provided.

Commission

❋ What are the steps you can begin to take that will enable you to walk out of measure into fullness?
❋ What must change in your heart first? How must your thinking be aligned next? Use the space provided to process your way forward in a way that causes you to smile, laugh and develop a sense of wonder!

Personal Notes

Alignment Creates Breakthrough

There are two battles we face in any personal issue. The first is to become free, and the second is to stay free. We have all seen people who received a breakthrough but who did not maintain it. There is no breakthrough without follow-through.

There is a situation involving David that wonderfully illustrates this principle.

> *Now when the Philistines heard that they had anointed David king over Israel, all the Philistines went up to search for David. And David heard of it and went down to the stronghold. The Philistines also went and deployed themselves in the Valley of Rephaim. So David inquired of the LORD, saying, "Shall I go up against the Philistines? Will You deliver them into my hand?" And the LORD said to David, "Go up, for I will doubtless deliver the Philistines into your hand." So David went to Baal Perazim, and David defeated them there; and he said, "The LORD has broken through my enemies before me, like a breakthrough of water." Therefore he called the name of that place Baal Perazim. And they left their images there, and David and his men carried them away. Then the Philistines went up once again and deployed themselves in the Valley of Rephaim.*

Therefore David inquired of the LORD, and He said, "You shall not go up; circle around behind them, and come upon them in front of the mulberry trees. And it shall be, when you hear the sound of marching in the tops of the mulberry trees, then you shall advance quickly. For then the LORD will go out before you to strike the camp of the Philistines." And David did so, as the LORD commanded him; and he drove back the Philistines from Geba as far as Gezer. [2 Samuel 5:17-25].

Historically, the Valley of Rephaim is one of the places populated by the sons of Anak, who were giants. When Moses sent out the spies to look over Canaan (Numbers 13) they brought back a bad report regarding the land.

"The people who live in the land are strong and we saw the sons of Anak." (v 28). These people are too strong for us, we are not able to go up against them (v 31). It is a land that devours its inhabitants; all the people we saw are men of great size. We saw the Nephilim (sons of Anak) and we became like grass-hoppers in our own sight." (v 32-33).

Rephaim is a place of stubborn resistance. It represents fear, intimidation, unbelief, and a poor self image. It is a place of past defeats and accommodations with the enemy.

It represents in our lives the areas of our heart that still stubbornly resist the grace of God - areas of constant defeat where we give way to sin. It describes a poor self image, where we cannot take ourselves seriously; therefore no one else can see us differently. We are a visual aid to low self esteem.

Rephaim symbolizes areas where we have little or no control, and we blow it on a regular basis. However it is also the place that God has chosen for breakthrough. It can become the opportunity to believe God in the battle for personal territory.

The first rule of warfare is that we cannot take ground from the enemy if he has ground in us. Hence the message of Jesus, Paul, and James. *"The prince of this world has come but has nothing on me"... Jesus (John 14:30). "Give no place to the devil"...Paul (Ephesians 4:27). "Submit to God, resist the devil, and he will flee from you"...James (4:7).*

Rephaim can also typify the life of believers who have stopped responding to the Lordship of Christ. The enemy has them convinced that nothing will happen; nothing will change. Therefore people learn to accommodate their sin and weakness. They learn to live with it, which means that everyone else has to settle for less in their relationship with that person. When we fail to respond to the overtures of God, we remain the product of all our yesterdays.

Warriors fight unbelief. They are committed to a relationship that trusts and to a lifestyle of faith. Warriors love people enough to not allow them to settle for anything less than overcoming. Warriors recognize that they have a spirit of breakthrough and therefore want to pursue the certainty of victory. They have become accustomed to fixing their eyes on Jesus. Like David, their heart is fixed.

In warfare, it is one battle to take ground and another battle to hold that ground. Jesus said, *"Occupy till I come," [Luke 19:13]* in the parable about a nobleman who went away and resourced his servants to do business in His absence. It's a story about being fully engaged and totally occupied with the matter at hand. Once we have taken territory, we must be about the business of keeping it and occupying it wisely.

If we concede it to the enemy, then he re-occupies it for his own agenda. Jesus must take up residence in our hearts, or we will lose His Presence by default. By His death and resurrection, Jesus has broken the power of the enemy once and for all. Now He must take up occupation of our lifestyle. Our ongoing obedience is key.

Each battle has different strategies, objectives, and tactics. Not every fight is the same. In the first battle at Rephaim, the enemy controls the ground, and there is a need for direct confrontation. In the second battle, David controlled the ground and could therefore fight in a different way as the Lord led him.

A breakthrough means to a) force a passage through a barrier or restraint and b) to open the way for new developments to occur. There is a breaking out and a breaking in.

We break out of things that bind and hold us back. We push through areas of defeat and overcome. We take on the issue of our poor self image and develop a new identity.

We break into an anointed lifestyle that provides us with the victory and the power to live as God intends. Our relationship with God goes to a new level of passionate intimacy. We begin to develop gifts, anointings, and presence that not only empower us but also have an impact on other people.

The purpose of warfare to a spiritual warrior is that the majesty and supremacy of Jesus can be realized. Warfare empowers us to demonstrate the power of God because the enemy should bring out the best in us. Conflict, whether it is human or spiritual, will always release the anointing.

As the enemy attacks, we get to establish oneness of heart and unity of purpose. Warfare enables us to produce the next tier of warriors who can learn to hold onto the vision. Hostile action can establish the purpose we are here to accomplish. We also get to know the areas of weakness and learn how to develop them into overcoming. We are enfranchised to restore what was stolen.

Often the greatest outcomes are achieved in time of challenge, confrontation, and contesting. Warriors have developed an internal fortress where

Jesus reigns. It is unthinkable that God would commit us to a battle and not resource us for the fight.

Of course, it is incredibly important that we really understand and develop the astonishing Good News of the Gospel in all its fullness and glory. We are betrothed to a King and must behave accordingly. God is not reluctant to bless us. He is our place of refuge and shelter. When we are placed in warfare situations, we must always return to our source in God. It was in the refuge where David wrote Psalm 91 about the secret place of the Most High.

To a warrior, warfare is a good test of their resolve and their capacity. When the enemy attacks our weakness, the Father is teaching us to live in our strengths. He is our stronghold, our life, our truth. We are learning how to fight His way.

The issue in each battle is **how** do we fight in this particular conflict. What specifically are the weapons of warfare that God is choosing? Sometimes the weapons are simply rest and peace - not allowing ourselves to become anxious or worried. Other times the weapon may be worship, praise or joyous celebration - to be occupied with God in the face of the enemy.

Always, it is the truth of who God is in Himself and in who He is choosing to be for us in that particular moment. He fills all things with Himself.

We must come to a place where we can break through over the past so that we cannot be dictated to in the present by previous events. We must receive the promise of God again - to know that we can go up against the evil one and that God will give that territory into our hand. He loves to restore and rebuild. He loves to teach us to rise up in our inner man. He loves to prove that He is with us.

This is Holy Spirit territory. He excels at all He does. He does everything with such grace, kindness, and innate cheerfulness. His exuberance for life and outrageous enthusiasm for us makes Him the ideal life companion, tutor, and friend.

What is established in us regarding the truth, through confrontation and contesting, now forms the base of operations launched against the enemy.

Warriors love the Holy Spirit. They receive Him as He is meant to be received - as Lord. Jesus is the undisputed, incredible, incomparable Lord over the church. The Holy Spirit is the unparalleled Lord within the church. His genius for life, truth, and warfare is legendary. He is a master strategist, a warrior who has never tasted defeat.

Warriors know that there will always be opportunities to fight. They receive them from the Lord! We learn from the Spirit the ways of war. We are meant for breakthrough. All public victories are preceded by private ones. The Holy Spirit shares in all our life events to make us like God. We are made in His image so that we can face each day as He does - joyful, peaceful, and powerful.

Warriors know the art of receiving breakthrough. They are familiar with it in their own lives first, and then through their ministry to others. War is concerned with taking territory. First, we must reclaim our inner territory. Secondly, we must retake our streets, cities, states, and then the nations.

Heaven is a breakthrough community. We, as its citizens, are consumed with a passion to bring heaven to earth - on earth as it is in heaven.

Assignment

* What is your next place of personal breakthrough? Is there any place in your life that is resisting the grace of God?
* Is your self esteem on the same level as the Holy Spirit's confidence?
* What is the promise of God over you as you contest the inner territory of your life? Keep a personal record of your break out, in the space provided.

Commission

* Look around you: at family, friends, fellow travelers in Jesus. What breakthrough do your companions need at this time?

❊ What can you be for them? How will you help them to break out of their restraints and break into their anointing and provision?
❊ Devise a process, a step by step guide to aid them in breakthrough. Teach it, model it, and mentor in it.

Personal Notes

Warriors look for Treasure

The key to any spiritual victory is to think like the Lord. Perception is everything. Spiritual warriors need to be God-conscious. The difference between Elisha and his servant in 2 Kings 6 was that one was focused only on earthly issues while the other was concerned with what God was doing. Elisha saw beyond the natural realm, and his perception was the difference between death and breakthrough.

As we become God-conscious, our spiritual awareness will expand our perceptions in the spiritual realm. Nowhere is that more needed than in the art of people development. Warriors work with the Holy Spirit. They are doing whatever He is doing; their actions are aligned with His intentionality. Their speech also reflects His heart. Alignment is about developing a relationship with the Holy Spirit based on His affinity for people.

The Holy Spirit has a natural liking for people. He is so brilliant at understanding people! He knows their longings and desires. He sees the thoughts and intentions of their heart. He is familiar with their struggle, weakness, and yearning to be better.

Because Jesus has so thoroughly dealt with sin on the Cross, the Holy Spirit is released to support our journey from the present to the future. He is happy and willing to apply this Cross to any present/past dilemma that we may face as we proceed towards breakthrough. It is in the matter of who we are becoming that He particularly excels.

He knows who we are now, in the present, and He links that person with our future destiny and identity. In Genesis 18: 17-18 the Lord says:

> *"Shall I hide from Abraham what I am about to do* **since** *Abraham will surely become a great and mighty nation, and in him all the nations of the earth will be blessed?"*

The word "since" means: for the reason that. It is also a preposition that denotes the action to be taken in the intervening period between the time mentioned (now) and the time under consideration (when Abraham will indeed become a great and mighty nation).

Because of Abraham's future destiny, he can be a part of what the Lord wants to do in the present. The Holy Spirit has a particular genius for present/future living. One of His gifts is prophecy, which is the art of encouragement, not only for the present, but also for empowering us in our future identity.

We have two relationships with God: who we are in the present, and who He says we are in the future. Jesus occupies the space between those two identities as He stands in the gap, interceding for us before the throne [Hebrews 7:25].

31

We are so much more beautiful than we know, and more powerful than we realize. Often when we are solely preoccupied with the present, we can lose sight of where we are going and who we are becoming. We get caught up with negatives, burdened by our sense of lack. At this point, we need someone to tell us who we are in Christ. We need people to remind us of our true identity. We need our companions to speak into our future destiny. Someone needs to see the treasure and not just the earthen vessel.

The answer to our present is the future. Most of our current situations have a bearing on our future development: They are about training for reigning, learning about authority and power, gaining in wisdom and character, putting off the self and putting on Christ, developing gifts and abilities that will sustain us for the times ahead.

We are not locked into the here and now. We have a direction, a vision, a sense of ourselves beyond the present. Life in the Spirit is very different than life in the natural. It is so much more! Life in the natural is concerned with future goals and how we move towards them. The gap between aspiration and achievement is development. We try to upgrade our performance so that we can become someone.

Life in the Spirit works differently. We already are someone in Christ. We are not trying to extricate ourselves from an old lifestyle. Jesus has already done that. We are dead in Him to our past. Life in the Spirit is simply about letting go of a life that no longer works. We are a new creation, a new person already in Christ. We are in the wonderful process of discovering who we already are in Him. We do not become a new person by changing our behavior. We discover the person we already are in Christ and behave accordingly.

When the Lord shows up in our life, He has a wonderful way of declaring to us how He already sees us. He knows both who we are now and who we will become. Who we are now is earthed in our personality. This is a mixture that is both positive and negative.

Personality is the integrated organization of soul and body. It is the combination of psychological, intellectual, emotional, and physical attributes that have shaped our upbringing, training environment, and modeling into a learned behavior that is both positive and negative.

Our positive personality contains the values that we have learned in life where we have become optimistic, trusting, willing to learn, and brave. We have developed capabilities that enable us to try, take risks, be open to challenge, and become self aware, uncritical, and open. We live by principles and values that empower us to be faithful, consistent, integrous, and worthy of trust.

Our negative personality is often shaped by disappointment, humiliation, betrayal, and the bitterness of life. We can find ourselves subject to discouragement and disillusion. We develop a victim mentality. We become cautious, pessimistic, and judgmental. We are fearful, hesitant, prone to deception, believing the worst, unworthy and entirely too self-conscious. We have a fear of man, being wrong, and looking stupid. We take comfort in the familiar and avoid taking risks.

When the Lord shows up in our life He tells us who we are becoming. Our true identity is made up of our personality and our persona. God loves to reveal our persona, how we are known in heaven. Persona is linked to the journey of our relationship with God.

Gideon is hurt, angry, and afraid. He is hiding out from the Midianites in a wine press, making bread, trying to keep body and soul together. He is disillusioned and has issues that bother him about his country and the Presence of God [Judges Chapter 6].

When the Lord shows up, He does not speak to any of those things. He is not here to deal with Gideon's personality, but to introduce to him his persona. Our persona is how we are known in heaven.

"The Lord is with you, O valiant warrior." Gideon meets this revelation in his personality...

"Why has all this happened? Where are the miracles? The Lord has abandoned us."

The Lord does not respond to personality, He reciprocates with more persona. *"Go in this your strength and deliver Israel from the hand of Midian. Have I not sent you?"*

Once again, Gideon counters through his negative personality. *"How shall I deliver Israel? Look, my family is the least in our tribe, and I am the youngest in my father's house."*

Again the Lord ignores Gideon's personality and speaks to his persona. *"Surely, I will be with you, and you shall defeat Midian as one man."*

There are three levels to our persona. These are: elevated status, legal authority, and permission to overcome. We are known in heaven. Our identity, as God sees it, gives us an authority over any opposition. We are resourced in our persona and given permission to overcome any obstacle.

I have two granddaughters, Evelyn (2 ½) and Annabelle (2 months). Both are developing their personalities. Both get their needs met every day by loving parents, Mark and Sophie. Neither child has to do anything to get their needs met. Indeed, at this time it is utterly impossible for Annie to do anything. Children get their needs met. Mature people receive their inheritance. We are all children of God learning to become Sons of God.

Our persona is given so that we can grow into maturity. Inheritance is attached to persona. How we are known in heaven is combined with how we are resourced from heaven. *[*For a more detailed account of persona and personality, listen to CD's on "Truest Identity" and "Maintaining Our Inner Compass", available from Brilliantbookhouse.com].*

Spiritual warriors live in their persona. They walk on earth in the language of heaven. They journey with heaven's perception of them. Therefore their own language and perception is taken straight out of the dynamic of their own relationship with the Lord.

Warriors look for treasure in people. They speak to the treasure and call it up. They remind people of who they are in Christ. They are a positive influence on people because they inspire people to become more. They have a new significance, an ability to see people and circumstances with a fresh spiritual, and therefore, mental approach.

Warriors are more prophetic, able to see what is hidden both underneath and behind the issues facing people. God-conscious individuals are especially gifted at seeing the treasure buried in the people around them. They see the good with a startling clarity, and their heart is moved with compassion and exuberance. The Holy Spirit has astonishing enthusiasm for people. When we see and listen from our heart (inner man), then we experience the heart of Jesus flowing through us.

> *The eyes of your understanding being*
> *enlightened; that you may know what is the*
> *hope of His calling, what are the riches of the*
> *glory of His inheritance in the saints.*
> *[Ephesians 1:18].*

The Father has an enlightened view of us in Christ. He looks at us affectionately through the lens of Jesus. The Holy Spirit empowers grace in our lives. Grace is the wonderful reality of God's loving-kindness towards us that compels us to feel loved as we are walking out our salvation in the goodness of God. We are loved always, and in all circumstances - in our strength and growth, in our weakness and struggle, in our learning and not getting it, in our awareness and maturity, in our freedom and in our hang-ups. Coming to Jesus and being with the Holy Spirit enables us to fully embrace the Father's love. We have three truly awesome, majestic, incredible, astonishing people who love us with great affection, intention, and power. Our low self esteem has no chance of survival.

I lost my poor self image a while ago. I have no feelings of shame, condemnation, unworthiness, or low self esteem. They simply cannot exist in the love, mercy, grace, and affection of God. There is no place for them, just as there is no place for the devil.

I am wonderfully and superbly loved. Each member of the Godhead takes time to upgrade me constantly to the next level of their enlightenment. They inhabit a place of shining brilliance where the light of the truth of how they see me is so powerful; it blinds me to anything else.

As I respond to what the Holy Spirit is doing, the affection of God for me is so strong it lifts me into a place in His heart.

Also, as I fail to respond to what the Holy Spirit is doing, the affection of God for me is so strong it lifts me into a new place in His heart. The Lord is consistent, faithful, and unchanging. My performance or non performance is quite irrelevant. He remains the same: yesterday, today, and forever.

He loves because He is love. He sees the treasure in me because He put it there. Jesus is in me (treasure), and I am in Him (treasured). Brilliant!!

Authentic spiritual warriors are treasure seekers. They see past the earthen vessel. If we were digging in our garden and found an old chest, we would want to see what was inside. We would be curious to discover something, excited and enthusiastic. Upon opening it and seeing the treasure, we would not close the lid to examine the box. Delight would fill us. We would be gripped by elation and absolutely thrilled at all the possibilities that the treasure could open for us.

When the Lord shows us the treasure in people, we are fascinated by what we see. Our hearts are overlaid by His, and we speak from the place of His deep affection.

In prophecy, people are caught up in the love of God. New Testament prophecy elevates the Christ life within people. We edify, exhort, and comfort people when we graciously challenge their hearts with the beauty of Jesus.

Warriors do what God is doing. We look for treasure and speak to it. We declare people's persona, and we help them to eradicate shame, condemnation, and a poor self image.

Assignment

❋ What would it be like for you to see yourself through the lens of Jesus?

❋ Sit down with a friend and agree to be one another's treasure seeker.

❋ Pray over them, ask the Lord questions about them, see them positively in the scriptures. What vision does the Father have of them?

❋ When you are ready, write them a letter from the Father [best handwriting!] that outlines who they are in Jesus and what treasure they have.

Commission

❈ Train your heart in the goodness of God.

❈ What would it take for you to see everything (good, bad or ugly) through the goodness of God?

❈ When we exercise ourselves in Godliness, we are learning to walk and talk in the goodness of God.

❈ Think of the people who are around your life on a regular basis. Name them in the space provided. What can you say and do that would influence them to feel the love of the Father?

❈ Please note: The harder their heart towards you, the more you are going to change for the better as you practice treasure hunting with them; that is as you speak to their treasure, regardless of their behavior, something has to change!!

If not them, then surely it has to be you!!! Yahoo! As the Lord is faithful, you can become consistent and unchanging. You are not treasure hunting in order to make people better: you are a treasure seeker because it's a brilliant way to live, regardless of outcomes.

Personal Notes

Intuition

Raising our awareness of what God is doing also produces a heightened level of intuition, the instinctive ability to pinpoint something. A strong sense of intuition allows us to take an ax to the root of the trees around us, rather than focusing on the branches. We learn the cause, not the effect. We gain the ability by doing the simple things in the name of the Lord -- things like meditation, praise, prayer, and other disciplines.

By waiting on God, listening to Him, and spending time with Him, our focus is strengthened. God-conscious spiritual warriors do not allow anything to take their focus off the Lord. We use bad circumstances, as well as good, to advance the Kingdom. Nothing bothers the enemy more than seeing what he meant for evil being used for good. The harder he pushes, the more ground he can lose to a warrior.

Warriors push back using their praise, rejoicing, and celebration. It is by our focus on God that the enemy is defeated. When we are in a fight, God commands all of our attention. The enemy would love us to focus on him in warfare. *"Our eyes are upon you,"* is the response of a warrior committed to majesty. Read 2 Chronicles, chapter 20, and spend time thinking about the astonishing prayer of

Jehoshaphat when outnumbered and facing annihilation [v 5-12].

We only face the enemy when God commands. Our focus is the majesty of the Father, the sovereignty of Jesus, and the supremacy of the Holy Spirit. The fullness of Godhead produces a weight of glory because the sum total of the august nature of God is revealed. We need to bask in His glory, allowing the brightness of it to overwhelm us, and the lightness it creates to fill our hearts.

This is a mystery to me: how the weightiness, the heaviness of God's glory can produce such lightness in our spirit. When we touch glory, we are filled with joy, and our heart becomes light and carefree. There have been times in my devotional experience when the glory of God has filled up my inner space and the lightness of heart and life have been so profound that it seemed all my bones turned to water and I had no ability to stand. I felt that I could float away. Every ability for negativity just left. I could not even imagine what anxiety, worry, fear, and doubt would feel like. I radiated joy. I was entranced by love, loving, and being the beloved. A peace so great filled my heart and mind, and I was completely and utterly relaxed.

Experiences with God are not one-time events. They are an introduction to a way of being with Him in life. They are permission to become in His image what He is like consistently. Our normality comes under pressure from His beauty. Life in the Spirit advances our experience continually.

What we feel is exceptional can now become typical. What is remarkable about God can become conventional by experience. We are being changed from glory into glory. Therefore all change is glorious. When heaven comes to earth, we are subject to a higher imprint of life. We are taken up, affected by majesty.

We come to a place where we look for sovereignty. It is always present in the person of Jesus. Every circumstance becomes vulnerable to our intuition about the nature of God. We are not intimidated by the enemy; we are too busy being fascinated by Jesus.

It is normal for us to be filled with God. It is our usual lifestyle. He fills all things with Himself. We become vulnerable to His goodness and loving-kindness. Our thinking becomes radically consistent with God's nature. We become intuitive about Him. We develop ability in the Spirit to understand and work things out by the inherent nature of Christ within.

He lives in us. We have the mind of Christ. We are filled to overflowing by the Spirit. The natural mind cannot comprehend the things of the Spirit, but we have the mind of Christ. All knowledge must contain an actual experience, or we have learned nothing in life. If what we say we know has not

44

changed our behavior, then we do not know it. We have not encountered it.

All knowledge in scripture must lead us to divine encounter, otherwise we are ever learning but never coming to a knowledge of the truth [2 Timothy 3:7]. The truth must set us free to walk with God differently. Our experience upgrades our wisdom. Encounter increases our intuition about who God is for us. We explore those things by living in that place of divine instinct. It is not always reasoned out beforehand, mostly that comes later, as we meditate.

Meditation is the art of thinking beyond our normal ability. It opens us up to the creativity of the Father and the wisdom of the Godhead. Meditation is a room in our hearts that has two doors; one door is knowledge, and the other, experience.

The rule of meditation is this: you must exit by the door opposite the one you entered. When we enter by knowledge, we must encounter God before we leave. He will give us revelation and wisdom, spiritual insights that open up our hearts to all that He wants to be for us. We enter into an experience of what He has just told us so that we **become** the truth in our life. Knowledge is cemented by experience.

When we enter by experience, we need knowledge to establish the truth effectively in our hearts. Part of that knowledge will be concerned with becoming the truth, developing the exceptional into the normal. Life is above tradition and is therefore served by it. As we change from glory into glory our thinking becomes less rational, more perceptive, more intuitive, and wise.

If we enter by experience and leave by it, we merely become exalted by God, but essentially unchanged. If we enter by knowledge and leave by it, our life is merely words in a notebook, and we remain unaffected.

What we encounter by intuition, we must learn to do by design. Knowledge and experience are two sides of the same coin.

Warriors live by encounter. They know that all of life in the Spirit is paradoxical, that is two apparently opposing ideas contained in the same truth. For example, we must die to live, give to receive, be last to be first. The Father requires knowledge with experience. It is what makes our spirituality authentic.

As we learn the ways of God we develop a Holy Spirit intuition about the nature of life in the Kingdom. In the most trying of circumstances we are able to focus on who God is, so that we can listen for His battle plan for the situation.

Reason and rationale are overrated – useful, but not essential, and mostly useful after the fact and not before. When intuition is minimized, we cannot move into the miracle that the Lord seeks to provide. Reason talks us out of encounter more times than it talks us into it.

Rationale looks for God through human provision. Intuition is dependent on the nature of who God is in relationship to our experience of heaven coming down. We can become so earthly minded that we have no encounter with heaven.

Warriors are people of encouragement. They have met the Lord in every circumstance of life, and it has become their tradition. Encounter, intuition and sovereignty are all linked together in a relationship that is full of love, laughter, and learning. This is the freedom of Christ. It is the Lord's doing, and it is marvelous in our eyes.

Assignment

❊ Read 2 Chronicles 20:5-12. Meditate on the prayer of Jehoshaphat.

❊ Explore his focus on the nature of God. What should your focus become for your own circumstances at this time?

❊ What confidence are you meant to experience in the Lord at the present moment?

❊ What does the Father want to do against the enemy in your present situation? What provisions are yours?

❊ How is He asking that you stand before Him in the current situation? Use the space provided to journal your responses.

Commission

❋ Read 2 Chronicles 20:14-19. Meditate on the prophecy of Jahaziel.

❋ What is the word of the Lord for your present situation?

❋ What is the process (series of steps) that you must take to experience an encounter with God's majesty?

❋ What is the attitude and approach that the Lord wants you to develop into a place of instinctive and intuitive response both for now and for the future?

❋ What will your response be to the move of God in terms of your joy and celebration as a lifestyle?

Personal Notes

Intensified Experience

The Holy Spirit loves consistency. He grows it in us by magnifying the wonderful nature of God. He will focus our attention on a single aspect of God's nature and magnify that truth for us.

My testimony is that God is the kindest person I have ever met. In 1991, the Father began specifically to teach me about His nature and my lifestyle, in order that I could be made in His image personally.

Whatever God is, He is relentlessly. He is relentless against the enemy. He is a persistent warrior-King determined to release His people from bondage into victory. His love is undeviating. His faithfulness is so perpetual all we can do is give in to it. His promises are unbroken. His joy continues unabated. His goodness is unstoppable. He sustains us with His own nature. He is relentless in the most amazing and surprising ways. He is wonderful so that we might become full of wonder.

As the Lord began to teach me about His kindness, I enjoyed the contact, the lesson, the experience. I simply assumed after a while that the lesson would cease. I would "get it," and God would move on; I would know the truth, be set free, and He would show me something else.

I "got it", loved it, had some great experiences of God's kindness. I found myself restless to move on and learn something else of God's nature. The lessons continued, day after day, month after month until there was not a part of my life that had not received kindness. Still it continued, until every day was marked by a specific act or word of kindness.

I was confronted in the most loving, compassionate, humorous ways about His loving-kindness. I laughed, I cried. It went so deep that I began to change. I began to speak kindly and act kindly towards others. I started to plan acts of kindness. I prepared kind words to speak deliberately into the lives of people. I developed a reservoir of kindness in word and deed. I gave kindness away at every opportunity. I became kindness.

Today, nearly 18 years (at time of writing) later, I am still receiving daily experiences of the Father's loving-kindness. We live in this space together. He is kind, and so am I.

Of course He has taught me other aspects of His nature. I am relentlessly loved. His unbroken love has broken my heart. His loving pursuit of me has washed away every bitter, humiliating experience of treachery and betrayal that I have been exposed to in human relationships. When the Father rebuilt my heart, it was bigger. That is still a mystery to me.

I had not realized how our lives are defined by negative experiences. Throughout the experience of God's relentless love, I kept expecting it to end. It was for a time and a season. Some things are for times and seasons, except for the nature of God. That is timeless, eternal, and persistent. He is relentless in the most beautiful way.

I thought that my behavior would lessen love. However, when I acted badly, love would intensify [Romans 5:20]. I thought that God was human and discovered He was divine. I was trying to make Him into my image; and when He broke my heart, He began the process of making me to be like Him.

On top of relentless kindness, He taught me about love in the most persistent manner. A few years later He began also to teach me about rest. When God teaches, He talks, acts, and moves in us consistently, until our experiences shape our thinking, perception, and behavior.

His relentless pursuit of rest and peace in me has brought me to a place of tranquility that astonishes me. I can bring myself to peace in around fifteen seconds. Rest is a way of life for me now, a normal fixture and feature of who I am in Jesus. Currently I am learning about relentless joy. I can feel my heart turning, softening, yielding to the persistent quality of the Father's joyful disposition.

Joy is eternal, everlasting. It does not depend on anything happening to cause God's happiness. He does not need a reason to be happy. His nature is persistent. Whatever God is, He is in fullness and abundance. When He talks to us, it is for the express purpose that His joy would rub off on us. *"These things I have spoken to you, so that My joy might be in you and that your joy may be made full." [John 15:11].*

Imagine what it is like to hear the voice of God who is incredibly happy. Imagine the effect that the sound of consistent happiness can have on a human heart. Then we are getting close to what we can live within constantly. With God every experience is intensified.

Revelation is not just about disclosure [John 16:13]. It is not just primarily concerned about communicating a truth. That truth must become real in our experience. Truth is incarnational. God always works from the whole to the particular. He applies all of His truth to specific areas of our life that require development. It is not enough for Him to change our behavior. He is not concerned to modify our conduct. He wishes to make us exactly like Him in each area of our life.

Truth sets us free when we become the living embodiment of it - when all our thoughts, words, and actions are so synchronized that we have effectively become the living word. As He is, so are we, in this world.

When we fail to preach truth as an incarnational experience, then we are merely communicating information about God. We are acquainting people with God; we are not immersing them in His nature. Proclamation is the art of declaring who the Lord is and that we have full permission to enter in and become that in Him. All teaching leads to encounter. Without personal engagement, we cannot be changed.

Informational teaching gives people pointers. It gives them things to do: "Follow these steps, and you can change yourself." This is nothing more than a glorified self-help program. People do not apply truth to themselves. The Holy Spirit relates truth to us. He brings us to a place of connection with Jesus where His relationship with us empowers us to be made in His image. Truth is a Person. *"I am the Way, the Truth, and the Life."* The truth is the Word made flesh.

The truth is a Person made real in our experience. Truth is relational and therefore incarnational. When we teach or preach incarnationally, then we are deliberately working with the Holy Spirit relationally, to draw people into an environment where they can experience the Presence of God in the spoken word.

Such teaching creates hunger, desire, and yearning. It opens people's hearts to all the possibilities of the nature of God. Blessed are those who hunger, for they shall be filled.

Imagine talking about food with people. Then imagine talking about food that is prepared, cooked, and available. In the first, we can share a recipe and invite people to picture the meal. In the second, we can share the recipe and invite people to taste and see. It's an intensified experience!

The Holy Spirit magnifies the Lord. He adores Jesus and loves to enlarge His appearance in our eyes. As He intensifies the Presence of Jesus to us, we find ourselves going beyond appropriating principles to actually encountering the One who is present.

We can become what the Holy Spirit is magnifying to us concerning God's nature. It drives us into a deeper relationship with Him. We are shaped by His Presence, chiseled and sculpted into His likeness.

Whatever the Holy Spirit magnifies to us will intensify our experience of the Lord. The weight of revelation will tell us the power of our experience. That is, it also denotes the volume of our permission.

When the Holy Spirit magnifies Jesus, the permission increases for us to become as He is. We get to discover the measures of God that make up His fullness. All truth about God's nature has four applications which are: length, breadth, height, and depth [Ephesians 3:16-21].

Oh, the lengths that God has gone to and will go to in our lives to empower us with love! The breadth of the scope of His love is astonishing. The heights to which love will take us, gives us a vision of the overall splendor of His nature. The depth at which He moves at in our lives is incredible. We feel overwhelmed by the majesty of His abundance. It is beyond even our imagination. It is too big for our mind to get to grips with that kind of reality.

Intensified experience leaves us breathless with anticipation. What next? Majesty provokes a different level of encounter.

Assignment

❋ What is the Lord working on in your life at this time?

❋ What does He want to be for you in this area that will open you up to Majesty?

❋ What encounter is the Holy Spirit seeking to provoke in your heart?

❋ Ask, and it shall be given. Keep on joyfully asking. It will surely come.

Commission

❋ What aspect of His own nature is the Father teaching you at this time?

❋ Define the attitude and approach of the Holy Spirit as your life coach, tutor, and facilitator.

❋ What encounter must you have with that specific aspect of God's character and personality?

❋ Listen to the Holy Spirit as He magnifies Jesus. Allow yourself to be drawn into that place of Majesty.

❋ Journal your thoughts and experiences in the space provided.

Personal Notes

Led by the Spirit

Being conscious of what God wants to do aligns us with Him and builds our resistance to the schemes of the enemy. As we resist what the devil wants to do, a desire forms to utterly defeat him. A passionate love for Jesus, combined with an intense hatred of the enemy, pushes us into alignment with the Holy Spirit. In the busyness of everyday life, we can sometimes drift into spiritual unconsciousness, sleeping through everything God is doing around us. But the Holy Spirit can bring us back in a split second; we just have to ask Him.

When the Holy Spirit is active within us, the fruit of self-control will always neutralize our flesh. We follow the Holy Spirit – He doesn't follow us. We are learning to be led by Him, especially in character issues. God wants us to live in an internal calm that produces harmony that flows to other people.

The oil of the Holy Spirit is indispensable for us. It keeps us moving forward, aligned with God's purposes. It is through alignment that we prove ourselves ready for more. He does not respect incompatibility. The Holy Spirit has too much purposefulness to be sidetracked by our intransigence. Often when we resist God's grace, He allows us to be diminished simply by not giving us more anointing. The level of anointing we currently possess can be reduced by lack of forward momentum. As we know from Matthew, Chapter 25, it is totally embarrassing when the oil runs out!

We are each responsible for our own alignment. We need to cultivate the joyful discipline of being led by the Spirit. No one can take our alignment from us, but we can choose to let it go. We should not rely on other ministries to supply the oil of anointing over our lives. We cannot keep relying on other people to give us revelation; we can get it for ourselves. Aligning with God is our own responsibility.

At a conference in Iowa, a man asked me to pray for the anointing of God to be restored. I asked him how he had lost it in the first place. His reply was that it did not matter now. Something had caused him to lose it a long time ago, and he wanted it back. The only person who can rob us of the anointing is us! The enemy will help us, of course. However, we have let go of God's provision. We can do that by default or deception. In default, we allow ourselves to be robbed because we are too casual with what the Father has bestowed. If we do not value what the Father has given, we will let go of it.

We can also be deceived by the enemy into allowing the anointing to diminish. We allow circumstances to increase until we are made small. We feel like a grasshopper facing the giants [Numbers 13: 32-33]. The enemy can magnify too.

Think of a car without oil. Now, think of an engine with the oil plug removed. We pour oil in, and it flows straight out. Unless the plug is restored, all the oil in the world has no effect.

Unless we repent of the specific reason that caused us to lose the anointing, we cannot be adequately re-filled. When I asked the man to consider his place of repentance, he declined and became angry. There are no shortcuts in the Kingdom of God. We cannot get around the work of the cross.

Assignment

* Have you lost anything?
* If so, you have an anointing to get it back. Face up to the reasons that deprived you of God's Presence in the anointing.
* Give them to the Father in full repentance.
* Ask for a fresh infilling and keep on asking until encounter comes.
* If after several days the infilling has not materialized, go back to repentance and search your heart afresh. [Psalm 139:23-24].

Commission

* Take an hour out of your day and practice being God conscious. Involve Him in

everything! Choose the busiest time of the day or the least stressful.

❄ Journal what you discovered in the space provided.

❄ Take it up a notch. Add another hour and complete the process.

❄ The most important part is the enjoyment that both the Holy Spirit and you will receive!

Personal Notes

God Schedules our Conflicts

God will organize people and design events just to give us the opportunity to grow in the fruit of the Spirit and in His grace. When we are in alignment with Him, we see these opportunities for growth clearly. If we are out of sync, we usually respond too harshly.

1 Corinthians 2:9 makes us an important promise: *"Eye has not seen, nor ear heard, nor have entered into the heart of man the things which God has prepared for those who love Him."* God reveals things to us by His Spirit. Our own spirit can sense these deep things and learn what God has prepared for us. We should all stay in alignment with God so we can be conscious of our opportunities in crisis.

Difficult situations and people exist to develop us in the things of God. *"For we are His workmanship, created in Christ Jesus for good works, which God prepared beforehand that we should walk in them,"* as Paul wrote in Ephesians 2:10. He has prepared a life curriculum to teach us how to walk more deeply with Him. But when we are out of alignment, we can only see the hassle of these situations -- not the benefit.

Maintaining our alignment enables God to work in us. It keeps us fruitful in Him. Spiritual life is very simple: God decides what we are going to do, and we decide if we will obey Him. The creator decides; the created discovers. God knows what He intends for us; we decide if we will cooperate.

If we are to develop as warriors, we must know the difference between our training ground and our proving ground. We are given personal training for reigning in our own private lives and circumstances. We get to make choices that reflect who God is for us and what He is developing in us. Private victories precede public triumph.

The public arena of life and ministry is our proving ground where we get to establish our private overcoming. The Lord Jesus had plenty of opposition, both human and otherwise, who attempted to trick Him into responses and actions that did not reflect the heart of the Father.

It was just another day in the life of David when his Father asked him to take some provisions to his brothers who were with the army of Israel. To be sure, there would have been some excitement at going to a battlefront camp. It beats watching sheep!

David had no clue that he was about to be thrust into circumstances that would catapult him into fame. Everyone around him thought he was untried and untested. Goliath laughed aloud when David presented himself for the fight. He disdained David who in his eyes was just a kid with pretty boy looks [1 Samuel 17:42].

David had gone through a similar process in his own camp when he had offered to fight the Philistine.

> *"You can't fight him, you're just a youth. Goliath has been fighting for years, since he was your age." [v 32].*

David's reply demonstrated his alignment with God.

> *And David said to Saul, "Your servant kept his father's sheep, and when there came a lion, and again a bear, and took a lamb out of the flock, I went out after him, and smote him and delivered it out of his mouth; and when he arose against me, I caught him by his beard and smote him, and killed him. Your servant killed both the lion and the bear; and this uncircumcised Philistine shall be as one of them, for he has defiled the armies of the living God!" David said, "The Lord, Who delivered me out of the paw of the lion and out of the paw of the bear, He will deliver me out of the hand of this Philistine." And Saul said to David, "Go and the Lord be with you!" [1 Samuel 17:34-37].*

His private victories over the lion and the bear had put him into a place of practiced dependence on the Lord. God had scheduled his conflicts in order to prepare him for the future that He had in mind.

God allows in His wisdom what He could easily prevent by His power. When we are in a place of alignment we are touched by majesty. There is a confidence that runs alongside our dependence. We magnify Him. We are conscious of all that He is for us.

Warriors do not look for rescue; they want to complete their assignment. The outcome of our assignment is never determined by the assignment itself. We go into every assignment as victors already. The Victory is ours; the battle is the Lord's. Victory is predetermined by our private responses. When Jesus is Lord in the ordinary, everyday situations of life, then His overcoming nature rises up in times of extraordinary conflict.

We are victorious because of our learned dependency. We have a posture of strength which comes to us by intimate connection. This is why worship, rejoicing, and thanksgiving are so essential. It is the language of intimacy that becomes the spoken word of victory.

Intimacy fuels majesty. David, a man after God's own heart, saw a God that was greater than Goliath. We never allow our circumstances to be greater than our awareness of God. He is all in all. Conflict is about practicing our revelation of majesty and proving that it is real and powerful.

Conflict with the enemy is essential in the development of the Christ-life. What is born of God must overcome the world [1 John 5:4-5]. Jesus was manifested to destroy the work of the devil [1 John 3:8]. The world is literally the present condition of human affairs and systems that does not represent God and indeed may exist in opposition to His nature.

This would involve both secular and sacred institutions. Jesus confronted the religious system as much as He opposed the system of government that ruled the nation. The devil works in both the sacred and the secular to ruin people's lives, remove their freedoms, and oppress them through the rule of man.

We are all part of the conflict of the clash between the darkness and the light. It is important that we do not live in the shadows. We are part of a kingdom that is not of this world. We are ruled from a place outside of space and time. The rule of God is greater than the laws of man. The people of God have always been mishandled by the rule of man and nowhere is that more evident than in the church itself. Jesus stood against a religious system that disenfranchised people from personal freedom and intimate connection with the Father.

Conflict is a vital part of our spirituality and cannot be escaped if we are to grow up in all things in Christ [Ephesians 4:15]. We do not go looking for trouble; there is no need. It will find us when God is ready.

We have more important things to do than go looking for the enemy. As we live Godly and effective lives in Christ Jesus, the enemy will come looking for us.

The Father trains our hands for war and our fingers for battle [Psalm 144:1]. He schedules all our conflicts. He provides for them. He sets promises in place next to them. He teaches us the way of the warrior. He trains us in the art of overcoming.

Conflict is not just concerned with people. It is in how we overcome barriers, problems, and life situations. We are being prepared to know the goodness of God in the land of the living, so that we never know despair [Psalm 27:13].

We have conflict so that we may learn the way of peace. When all is going well, peace is never an issue. Indeed, we do not think of it. When conflict arises, peace is God's truest provision. Peace empowers us to overcome. He gives us peace so that we may then find courage to stand in the day of trouble.

> *"These things I have spoken to you, that in Me you may have peace. In the world you will have tribulation; but be of good cheer, I have overcome the world." [John 16:33].*

Assignment

❋   What is your present conflict about?
❋   What is the Father developing in you?

* What is your current training ground?
* In your situation what is the measure of rule that the Father is giving you over your old self?
* What is the place of dependency that you must experience?
* What is your private victory?

Commission

* Thank God for the conflict. Rejoice in who He is for you.
* Write down the blessings, favor, promises, and provision that are present in this current conflict.
* How will you stand before God and practice the art of overcoming?
* What is your current proving ground where the Father is establishing you as an overcomer?

Personal Notes

Your Emotions Reveal your Destiny

The Lord loves everything about us that He has created. We are made in His image, and it is very good. The Lord gave us emotions so that we could experience Him, the Kingdom, and life in the fullest way possible.

Our positive emotions create in us the opportunity to discover God, inspire other people, and open ourselves up to Jesus through the Holy Spirit. The Father gave us the gift of tangible feelings so that we could practice the art of living from our heart, with Him.

Feelings make us closer to God than thoughts. Positive emotions inspire trust, faith, and expectation. In all of His dealings with us, the Father will use our emotions positively to connect with us.

Obviously, negative emotions, left unchecked, are detrimental to our well being and our walk of faith. The Father has provided for us in this area. It is a part of the mission statement of Jesus in Isaiah Chapter 61.

The Spirit of the Lord GOD is upon Me, Because the LORD has anointed Me to preach good tidings to the poor; He has sent Me to heal the brokenhearted, To proclaim liberty to the captives, And the opening of the prison to those who are bound; To proclaim the acceptable year of the LORD, And the day of vengeance of our

God; To comfort all who mourn, To console those who mourn in Zion, To give them beauty for ashes, The oil of joy for mourning, The garment of praise for the spirit of heaviness; That they may be called trees of righteousness, The planting of the LORD, that He may be glorified. [Isaiah 61:1-3].

Jesus proclaimed two things in His mission statement: firstly, that the favor of the Lord was upon us and secondly, that vengeance was available against our enemy.

The favor of God trains and equips us to live from a place of expectancy in His goodness so that we can stand in Him, no matter the opposition. Vengeance is the anointing and ability to attract favor when we are under attack.

The way that the Holy Spirit does that is to teach us about divine displacement. The key word in this passage is the word "instead." It means in place of, or an alternative to something else.

Beauty instead of ashes. The oil of joy instead of mourning. The garment of praise instead of a spirit of heaviness. The Lord has made provision for our negative emotions. He displaces them with His own nature. In Christ, nothing negative may work against us. The enemy can use negative emotions against us, which is why the Father gave us a Comforter (literally someone who provides relief from pain and distress). The Holy Spirit soothes our hearts and brings his own innate cheeriness to us. He supports and encourages us constantly. He brings freedom out of every situation that vexes or annoys us.

When the enemy has one purpose, the Father has another instead. He means for the opposite to occur. We see the same sense in Romans 8:31-39. If God is for us, who can be against us? How will God not freely give us all things? Who will bring a charge against us? Who will separate us from the love of God?

Instead of being overwhelmed by what we are not, we can be overwhelmed by who Jesus is for us. We are not consumed by the negative; we are overjoyed at the opposite. The Holy Spirit teaches us to move in the opposite spirit to a negative. God can use the enemy to point out our provision. Whatever the enemy has planned, the Lord has planned an alternative instead! It is our heritage to move in the opposite spirit. Think the opposite, move towards it, and reposition for a blessing.

The ultimate vengeance on the enemy is that whatever he tries against us only succeeds in making us bigger, better, stronger. When under attack, we focus on what the Father is giving us permission to become.

The Father has planned for every eventuality. This is the grandest passion of His life: to make us into His image, to provide an eternal companion for His Son. Everything that we need to fulfill that destiny has already been granted to us. Green lights, everyone! Everything in line with His purpose is "yes and amen" in Christ.

Any experience we want that makes us into God's image has His fullest permission. Anything that makes us excellent adds to His glory. On our worst day, out of nightmare circumstances, when under insidious attack from people, or surrounded by a corrupt world and an implacable enemy, we can become partakers of God's divine nature.

Think of it: a life that cannot be stopped, a nightmare for the devil. The promises of God are so huge and have such intense value in the Kingdom; yet He gives them away so freely, so easily to us [2 Peter 1:2-4]. The Father will deny us nothing in Christ.

The work of the Holy Spirit is to cause us to rise up and occupy the Word, to be filled with Jesus, to live in fullness, and to think, pray, and speak out of His abundance.

All that we are is to be filled with all that He is in Himself. That obviously means that our emotions are a key part of God's dealings with us. His emotions are beautifully seen in His love, compassion, peace, gentleness, faithfulness, goodness, patience, grace, mercy, and joy.

His feelings for us are so powerful! It's an odd thing in the Evangelical world that the only time we truly talk about God's emotions is when we claim He is angry about something or someone. Yet God

Himself claims to be really slow to anger, even under the old covenant. Of course, He is not angry at all in the new covenant, having poured it all out on Jesus on the Cross. Jesus was separated so that now we can always be with God in this life [Romans 8:35-39].

I love His voice. I love the effect it has on me emotionally. The sound it makes in my heart. I love the sound that comes out of my heart when the sound of His heart touches me. It is the sound of purest joy, the sound of a deep, all encompassing happiness so profound that like a raging flood it carries all before it. When He speaks, my heart sings. The deposit He leaves in my heart is His own innate happiness. *"These things I have spoken to you so that My joy may be in you, and that your joy may be made full." [John 15:11].*

It was a good day for the demonic realm when the devil persuaded believers to have a cerebral relationship with God instead of a heart fellowship, when he caused people to equate knowledge only with understanding, but not experience. So theology became academic and lost its experience and vitality. Life in the Spirit gave way to a logical, rational, reasonable, and functional relationship with God that contained little intimacy and no supernatural, miraculous dynamic. Christianity became a religion, a dull, drab, boring, powerless, emotionless (unless we count anger) tradition.

I wonder if this is what James meant when he wrote about a wisdom that was devilish [3:15]; or what Timothy meant when he wrote about doctrines of devils? [1 Timothy 4:1]. Certainly there is no possibility of God being glorified in a powerless church; nor is there any chance of revealing the majesty and supremacy of Christ through people who are drab, dull, and lacking in astonishment. Certainly, we as Evangelicals need to repent and return to believing the whole Bible.

Saying that we have a relationship with God but not being able to feel His presence is too silly for words. No child would believe that, yet we adults talk about faith and believing as though they were the antidote to emotions.

How can we not feel faith? *"Faith comes by hearing, and hearing by the word of Christ." [Romans 10:17]*. How can we hear incredibly GOOD NEWS and not feel glad as we believe?

If, when God speaks to us and joy rises up, how will faith not rise up with our feelings of abundant joy? *"Now may the God of hope fill you with all joy and peace in believing, so that you will abound in hope [confident expectation] by the power of the Holy Spirit." [Romans 15:13]*.

We are filled with joy and peace in believing - faith and positive emotions, faith and attributes of God's nature, faith and feelings, acting together in partnership with the Holy Spirit!

Father loves our emotions. They were His gift to us so that we could live from our heart with Him. The emotions of the soul are subject to negativity, doubt, fear, anxiety, worry, panic, etc., because our soul and body are linked to the outside world. They have an external viewpoint subject to harassment by the enemy. Soul and body form the outer man, and our human spirit is made alive in Christ and is indwelt by the Holy Spirit. The inner man of the spirit only lives in the Presence of God. It has no external connection. Life flows from God within, through our spirit to the soul, and beyond. However, it does not flow back the same way. The soul cannot overwhelm the spirit. It can, however, take control of situations if our will permits.

The spirit within uses all the attributes of the Presence of God that mingles with our spirit. We are alive to God and all the possibilities of His nature [Romans 6:11]. NB [*For a more detailed understanding of soul and spirit, read Towards a Powerful Inner Life by Graham Cooke, available at Brilliantbookhouse.com*].

The Father loves our emotions. He connects trust and faith to His own emotions so that our inner man receives joy and peace in believing. He also uses emotions to connect us with our calling and destiny.

What you **love** is a guide to the gifting and influence that the Lord wants to bestow on you.

What do you love to talk about most? What gets you excited about the Lord and His Kingdom?

If everyone on earth was paid $20 per hour for work, regardless of the type of job; what would you be? A doctor, professor, CEO of a multi-national company, an actress, sports person, a janitor or a rat catcher - all paid the same. What would you do if money was not a factor? When you know that, you know something of who you are and what is your calling in the Kingdom.

Personally, I would be exactly what I am now - an intimate son, a loving friend who is paid to meditate, a worshipper, a man who loves to write, a reluctant public speaker who loves to talk about God, a trainer and equipper of people who adores the prophetic.

I love the prophetic. I love the fact that God speaks to us personally from His own mouth, through the scriptures, through people, circumstances, ministries, and especially through the Holy Spirit in the gifts of prophecy and wisdom.

I love the prophetic. That isn't surprising, I suppose, as I have dedicated my life to teaching it. I love watching people in tune with God and hearing His voice. I love seeing people find out the will of God for themselves. I love releasing people to hear the voice of the Lord. I am passionate about training people in the prophetic because I love it.

I began training people in prophecy in 1978 - a few workshops, some teaching, lots of question and answer sessions. In 1985, I started my first School of Prophecy, with a level 1 course. Now it is four courses spread over a number of years. I have people that I mentored who now teach levels 1 and 2, but I still love to teach people at level 1 who have never heard the voice of God.

More than thirty years have passed, and I still love that moment when people first hear God for themselves. I love that moment when God's heart and ours becomes one, and His voice breaks through into our conscious heart.

I wrote a book, *Approaching the Heart of Prophecy* that is designed to release people into the heart of God so that they can step into a place of receiving His voice.

What you are most happy about gives you power to inspire others. When our **joy** is full, we have an authority to lift people in the Spirit. Joy gives us influence that arouses desire in people. The angels came with glad tidings of great joy and inspired shepherds to leave their flock and go searching for a baby in the middle of the night!

I love the Holy Spirit. He is the happiest, most cheerful person I have ever encountered. It's possible to grieve Him, but incredibly difficult. Most of us will never manage it personally. The Godhead dwells in an environment of astonishing, everlasting joy. The Holy Spirit is a delight!

He is cheerful, exuberant, and amazingly enthusiastic about us. He loves His role as Comforter, tutor, and come-alongside friend. He gets to talk about Jesus (whom he adores) and equip us to fellowship with the Father.

He is an absolute genius at life, a brilliant mentor who knows everything. He has a wonderful sense of humor and is a powerful advocate and warrior. He is never fazed at circumstances but loves to lift us up to see more from His perspective.

He is a gorgeous, amazing paradox. He is recklessly cheerful and incredibly wise. He is full of majesty and yet astonishingly gentle. He is completely and radiantly Holy, yet comforts us in our struggles and lovingly teaches us the ways of righteousness.

He is inspirational, generous, kind, gracious, and endlessly patient in redeeming us to live in Christ. Talking about him fills me with joy. I love who he is in my life. When I talk about him publicly, a joy rises up in me that hopefully influences and inspires people to be filled with His presence. When I talk about the Holy Spirit, I feel the Christ within smiling through me. When the Holy Spirit talks to me about Jesus, I feel the pleasure of the Father and the Spirit. The Holy Spirit loves me to feel that I am the Beloved of God, accepted fully in Christ [Ephesians 1:6].

The **peace** of God gives us power to overcome [John 16:33]. In tribulation, there is a place of rest in the Holy Spirit who loves to manifest the peace of Christ and the peace of God that passes all understanding.

We are learning to fight from a place of rest and peace. To not be overwhelmed by fear, anxiety, or panic is a part of our heritage as people of Christ. Rest is a weapon. The enemy cannot penetrate our peace but he can be destroyed by it.

There will always be tribulation in the world. Peace works on us emotionally to create courage. The process of learning rest is wonderfully intoxicating. The Holy Spirit provides massive, ongoing encouragement that is so profound and amazing that worry, fear, and anxiety cannot live in our circumstances. They are banished by the sheer majesty of peace.

Peace releases an authority that commands total obedience. Peace makes us vulnerable to the Sovereignty of God [Mark 4:35-41]. The Holy Spirit is calm, unworried, untroubled by events. He is peaceful.

The astonishing truth (one of them) about God is that He can use anything to speak to us and help us. Everything is useful - a storm on a lake, a terrifying demoniac. Even death [John chapter 11] and taxes [Matthew 17:24-27].

The Father can also call on any negative emotions to help us and determine our future. For example, what we **hate** is a guide to what God has raised us up to deliver. I remember a few years ago, in a movie theatre in America, watching the Robert Duvall film *The Apostle.* It was an incredible film, with superb acting and a solid script, but I hated it. Duvall played a man who thought he could live any way he chose and still serve God. He was devious, manipulative, and occasionally violent, but also compassionate. He was locked in a struggle between the two sides of his personality.

I wanted to jump into the movie scene and confront him. I appreciated the acting, but the premise of the film annoyed me. At one point, I told God I was going to have to leave; the movie was making me too upset. In that moment, I felt God whisper into my heart, "Graham, this is everything I've called you to fight against." Immediately, I was refocused.

"Graham," God said, "I love the way you hate religiosity." The statement was true. I do not like performance Christianity. I dislike apathy and mediocrity. When I see it, I have to take it on.

The way we confront issues is vital. We are not fighting flesh and blood [Ephesians 6:12]. So there is no point in attacking people. As a guiding principle, when the enemy has a hold over God's people, he must be confronted indirectly.

We do that by talking about who God is for us. We must present a radiant idea of God so that people reach out for Him in divine exchange.

What we detest is a guide to that which God has called us to deliver. Every part of my anointing is to deliver the church from religiosity and back into compassion and into standing in the presence of God. I want reality. I hate double-mindedness.

Moses hated slavery. When he saw Egyptians beating Hebrews, his anger rose up. Why? There was a call on his life – even if he didn't know it at that precise moment – to be a deliverer. But this gift has a cost; what we most want to confront must be corrected in ourselves first. We cannot confront anything in other people unless we have already dealt with our issue. If we stray from this necessary order, we will be hurt. God will not tolerate an individual ignoring the plank in their own eye to pluck a speck out of someone else's.

Moses had to be trained in the wilderness in order for him to be changed and to bring change. If he had conceded and given up during that process, he would have forfeited his power. Other people may get weary of you banging the same drum, so keep the song but change the tune. Find creative ways of attacking the same problem. Remain focused on your call. If you read my books or listen to my teaching, you will know that I constantly address the same themes – but in several different ways. It takes wisdom and patience to attack things from every possible angle.

We have to be violent to wage the war God has laid out for us. If you are going to be in a fight, be in it to win. Show no mercy when you are attacking the enemy. Give grace to everyone but the devil. When he is on the floor, don't stop kicking him!

"Therefore, my beloved brethren, be steadfast, immovable, always abounding in the work of the Lord, knowing that your labor is not in vain in the Lord," Paul said in 1 Corinthians 15:58. *"And let us not grow weary while doing good, for in due season we shall reap if we do not lose heart," he* added in Galatians 6:9. We cannot change some thing unless we have a God-given hatred for whatever the obstacles are around it. Warfare must be implicit in everything we do.

We must have a compassion for people and a hatred for what holds them in bondage. Mercy for the individual, but rage against what imprisons them, sickness, injustice, poverty, addiction, racial prejudice, abortion – whatever it might be. Many things are wrong in our society, and they will not change unless someone compassionate and angry enough steps forward. Most of us have got plenty of compassion but not enough anger to confront issues. We need both.

Anger by itself is destructive. Anger and compassion together are productive. We have to wear this mantle, this anointing, this call in order to bring ourselves into alignment with God.

Agony is a clue to what we are called to restore. Nehemiah agonized over the state of Jerusalem. It led him to fast and pray until God gave him favor to restore the city's walls. His agony was a forerunner to his call. Likewise, Jesus agonized over the plight of the oppressed and blind, as His life passage, Isaiah 61 indicates. Jesus' agony for those oppressed by a religious system was a clue to what He was called to restore them to in relationship with His Father.

What makes us cry is a guide to what He will empower us to do. It is locked up inside of us and is released as we focus on God's plan. Jesus wept over Jerusalem; He was passionate about Israel. Paul felt the same grief, as we read in Romans 9:1-3:

I tell you the truth in Christ, I am not lying, my conscience also bearing me witness in the Holy Spirit that I have great sorrow and continual grief in my heart. For I could wish that I myself were accursed from Christ for my brethren, my countrymen according to the flesh, who are Israelites, to whom pertain the adoption, the glory, the covenants, the giving of the law, the service of God, and the promises; of whom are the fathers and from whom, according to the flesh, Christ came, who is over all, the eternally blessed God.

Our agony is a guide to the healing power God wants to give us. What grieves you today? Do you know you have the power to heal what you grieve over? When we are grieved, the prophetic word that will come out of our mouth will release people from bondage into freedom instead. Our grief can and will turn into an all-consuming passion in our heart. Some will call it obsession, but it is actually passion spilled over into sacrifice as we pour our hearts out to God.

In 1 Samuel, we read of Hannah's agony over her inability to have children. She wept bitterly, the Bible records in verses 15-16:

> *I am a woman of sorrowful spirit. I have drunk neither wine nor intoxicating drink, but have poured out my soul before the LORD. Do not consider your maidservant a wicked woman, for out of the abundance of my complaint and grief I have spoken until now.*

Hannah's grief gave birth to a life that became the most compelling voice in a nation where the word of the Lord was rare, and where vision was infrequent. Her grief gave birth to a solution. Likewise, Israel was barren and grieved God. Perhaps that is why He chose Hannah's agony to bring restoration. He saw His own anguish reflected in her tears. Hannah's agony was lifted when she became pregnant with Samuel, and that child later ended God's own agony with Israel.

Assignment

❊ What negative emotions are ruling you at this time?

❊ What would the opposite of that feeling, look and sound like to God, yourself, and others? What is God giving you instead?

❊ Ask the Father for favor on your emotions so that your heart can be more in tune with His. As you do so, promises will begin to come to you, and revelation of what God wants to be for you will rise up in your heart. Take notes in the space provided.

❊ Ask the Lord to speak to you in such a way that your emotions can connect with His faith.

Commission

❊ What do you feel strongly about?

❊ What you love is a guide to your gifting and influence with other people. Journal those thoughts.

❊ What you agonize over is a clue to what you are supposed to restore. What is that?

❊ What you hate gives you the power to deliver. Who and what are you empowered to set free?

❄ Identify your feelings and cross reference them with your permission in the Spirit. Claim your identity and your anointing!

Personal Notes

All Warriors are Anti-Religion

Heaven will always confront man-made spirituality. The best place for the enemy to hide is always in the guise of something spiritual. He masquerades as an angel of light. As we saw in the time of Jesus, He was constantly opposed by religious people who were fronting a system that they themselves had developed over many years.

In one confrontation with Jesus, He spoke to them about the fact that they "transgressed the commandments of God for the sake of their tradition" [Matthew 11:3]. Religious leaders invalidate the word of God for tradition's sake [11:6]. He called these leaders hypocrites who honor God with their mouth but not their heart, teaching their rules as though they were God's word [11:7-9].

The Pharisees were offended, but Jesus was unperturbed calling them blind leaders of the blind [11:14]. Matthew chapter 23 is a comprehensive direct attack on a religious system and the leaders who uphold that organization with all its practices and procedures.

If we are not leading God's people into direct encounter with Him, what is our leadership about? If people are not personally growing in Christ and fulfilling His Kingdom call, what are we developing? If our ministry is not raising up warriors and soldiers to fight the good fight, what type of believer are we producing? If our leadership is in control of how the church operates but it is not being effective in warfare, what is our control really cultivating?

Paul was faced in Corinth with people who wanted his ministry, seeing it as a title, a position, and a place to usurp. He talked about the need to cut these people off from the opportunity to be regarded as leaders and ministries.

He called them false and deceitful workers disguising themselves as apostles, and compared them to the devil, who also masquerades as an angel of light [2 Corinthians 11: 12-15]. The enemy loves to dress up and go to church. The best way to damage the people of God is to infiltrate their ranks and bring deception into their midst. If he cannot successfully overcome the people of God openly, he will seek to overcome them subtly from within. The enemy cannot stand against the truth of Jesus so he must undermine it with false doctrine of his own.

The Age of Enlightenment in the last millennium gave him the perfect opportunity to develop a rational, reasonable way to approach God. The supernatural was phased out as a part of dispensationalism. In this way, apart from salvation (which he knows he cannot control) people were guided away from hearing God's voice, taking steps of faith, and the delights of personal intimacy. God becomes less sovereign, more distant, intangible, and unknowable. He is relegated to being a mystery and a deity whose presence is really only felt by anger and judgment.

Introduce into that a legalistic, performance based spirituality in an atmosphere of doubt, fear, and dullness. The church universal is captured by a sanctuary-driven spirituality that centers on meetings, studies, and activities that do not provide direct encounters with a God of grace, love, power, and magnificence. People live by measure, not fullness - supposedly believing the Bible but actually living powerless lives below the level of Christ's identity and privilege.

Jude wrote about such infiltrations in his epistle.

> *For certain men have crept in stealthily [gaining entrance secretly by a side door]. Their doom was predicted long ago, ungodly (impious, profane) persons who pervert the grace (the spiritual blessing and favor) of our God into lawlessness and wantonness and immorality, and disown and deny our sole Master and Lord, Jesus Christ (the Messiah, the Anointed One). [v. 4].*
>
> *But these men revile (scoff and sneer at) anything they do not happen to be acquainted with and do not understand; and whatever they do understand physically [that which they know by mere instinct], like irrational beasts--by these they corrupt themselves and are destroyed (perish). [v.10].*

These are hidden reefs (elements of danger) in
your love feasts, where they boldly feast
sumptuously [carousing together in your midst],
without scruples providing for themselves [alone].
They are clouds without water, swept along by
the winds; trees, without fruit at the late autumn
gathering time--twice (doubly) dead, [lifeless and]
plucked up by the roots; Wild waves of the sea,
flinging up the foam of their own shame and
disgrace; wandering stars, for whom the gloom of
eternal darkness has been reserved forever. [v. 12-
13].
These are inveterate murmurers (grumblers) who
complain [of their lot in life], going after their
own desires [controlled by their passions]; their
talk is boastful and arrogant, [and they claim to]
admire men's persons and pay people flattering
compliments to gain advantage. [v. 16]
It is these who are [agitators] setting up
distinctions and causing divisions--merely sensual
[creatures, carnal, worldly-minded people],
devoid of the [Holy] Spirit and destitute of any
higher spiritual life. [v. 19].

Clearly, some of these people were
unregenerate in their behavior, and others were more
subtle in their desire to develop a spirituality more
earthly and natural.

The New Testament churches constantly had problems with false teachers, prophets, and wrong doctrine. This continues today in many forms.

The system must be directly confronted through the Holy Spirit. The people trapped in that system need to see what is oppressing them. There is a difference between religious leaders overseeing a church-going system that pays lip service to Jesus. A liberal approach to Christianity that robs people of personal engagement is easily recognized.

Then there is the more dangerously subtle version of church that majors on one person in the Godhead, misunderstands another by making Him in their image, and resolutely denies the ministry of the third member of the Trinity. People are not taught to hear God, ask for healing, power, or provision. They are not equipped to fight, worship, or develop on earth the lifestyle of Jesus. Theirs is an earthbound spirituality, not a heaven-based relationship.

Consequently these people do not have a personal revelatory experience of God that empowers them to live a life above their circumstances or see God as incredibly magnificent. Trapped in a functional paradigm of church, they are taught to serve but not encouraged to become sons of God. They are not trained in the glory or sovereignty of God; their joy is circumstantial, and their peace, often unsubstantial. They are more prone to experience doubt, anxiety, and fear before faith, courage, and breakthrough.

They do not live a life of celebration because they have never been taught the dynamics of ascended worship. They praise sporadically, give thanks weakly, and rejoice intermittently. They love God on their terms, not His. They live in the shallow places of Christianity because they have never been shown the deep places in Christ.

There is a difference between someone overseeing a religious system that binds people, and a person trapped in a place of spiritual mediocrity because they do not know that something profoundly better is available.

The first must be directly confronted as Jesus did with the Pharisees of His day. The second must be confronted indirectly and in a way that inspires them to see and know Jesus as Lord, not just as Savior. Such people are living under an atmosphere generated by a religious spirit.

A religious spirit dictates what people can believe and therefore experience. It controls the environment to create a resigned, unimaginative, and submissive spirituality that has little passion or energy.

One of the signs of a religious spirit is passivity, where people cannot rouse themselves in their own spirit and therefore allow themselves to come under something inferior.

The roots of it are in low self esteem, performance mindset, a feeling of unworthiness, and a sense that nothing much will change. There is an air of defeat and an atmosphere of powerlessness. People believe that Jesus Christ is Lord but have little experience of majesty.

In these circumstances, people mostly want magic, an impartation of God that will release them into freedom without them having to do anything in the process. Of course process is as much a part of our life as impartation and anointing. They form a paradox, a both/and, not an either/or solution to our dilemma. Our problem is that we have stopped responding to the majesty of God's love. We are not making ourselves vulnerable to His loving-kindness. Goodness still needs to get hold of us, and the joy of the Lord in working with us still needs to permeate our spirit.

If we go against a religious spirit directly we may find ourselves fighting on its terms. We draw attention to the "religious spirit," and it becomes more entrenched. A religious spirit looks for an offense so that it can erect a barrier and hunker down behind it.

A religious spirit disempowers people. Passivity and hopelessness travel together. When attacked, it can have the effect of people feeling "got at"; this makes them more weary and resigned, and the atmosphere hardens even more. The enemy loves docile believers. He works to render people compliant and inactive. When leaders and ministries do everything for people, they deliver them to a passive lifestyle of dependence on another source than the Holy Spirit. It is for freedom that Christ has set us free [Galatians 5:1].

Many people have gotten used to being no-one and doing nothing. They are children tossed to and fro [Ephesians 4:14]. A religious spirit creates the environment where people can look to someone other than their own relationship with God, and then it subtly makes it their fault if breakthrough doesn't occur - not enough faith, too little repentance, need for deliverance, gave up too soon, didn't pray hard enough, too weak, too passive, unbelief, double minded!!! These are just a few of the excuses that are banded around.

We are subtly turned around again to face our own performance as Christians, which further debilitates us. A religious spirit wants to control people's experience of God. Churches develop systems and structures that create an illusion of going somewhere but actually deny people the permission and the place to develop their own lifestyle, ministry, and relationship to hear God and obey. To move in the Spirit and grow up in Christ, we must restore people to the beauty of a radiant relationship with Jesus through the Holy Spirit.

We attack a religious spirit indirectly by proclaiming who Jesus is for us and declaring who He wants to be for us in our present circumstances. We must talk about glory. When we do, the drudgery of the religious-minded becomes apparent to them. The antidote to spiritual dullness is astonishment. When people open up to the radiant nature of Jesus, they begin to shrug off complacency. Like a flower cannot resist opening up to the sun, we cannot resist the joy and love of God.

Jesus is irresistible; and when we magnify Him, we create space for glory to descend. We must talk of God in superlatives so that our testimony in teaching impacts people and creates hunger.

A religious spirit cannot fight glory and radiance. It retreats into the shadow of rationality, a secular perspective without power. When we talk about the beauty of God, the hunger it creates to know Him in that way, begins to stir up desire. As people are set free to long for God again, passion begins to rise up. A determination to know God fully and a craving for His presence can be established. If we accompany that with wisdom, then a pathway will open up for people to follow. Wisdom is the understanding of how God thinks, perceives, and likes to work with us.

The beauty of our walk with God is that it is a relational process. It involves closure, conversion, and commissioning. We learn the pleasures associated with the Cross and its power to cause breakthrough. We learn the joy of simple change and the discovery of God's provision each day. We come alive to wonder, and we learn the authority that is part of identity.

We learn to be present/future and develop a lifestyle of celebration as we take charge of our surroundings. We see through the religious paradigm and move in the opposite spirit.

It's fun, throwing a religious spirit into utter confusion - fighting it on the terms permissible by the Holy Spirit, who is a compelling genius at this level of warfare.

Assignment

* Without passing judgment on your church experience, what must you take personal responsibility for in your spiritual walk with Jesus?
* Define your own passivity regarding your relationship with the Holy Spirit as a) Tutor b) Comforter and c) Equipper for ministry.
* What will you do to become more aware of your spiritual surroundings, and how you can upgrade the spiritual experience of your fellow believers?

Commission

* It is time to take your relationship with the Holy Spirit to a new level.
* Sit quietly over the next several days, allocating some meaningful time to thinking about a) what you want from the Father and b) what you sense He wants to provide regarding your fellowship with Him.
* Write a crafted prayer that fully expresses what you feel you want most from the Lord regarding a deeper encounter.
* Ask, and keep on (joyfully) asking!

Personal Notes

Signs of non Alignment

Spiritual warriors must be able to recognize when they are not living and moving in partnership with the Holy Spirit. The Lord has an impressive impact on our physical, emotional, mental, and spiritual states when He is Present with us.

Physically, it can be something as simple as loss of appetite. Tension and stress fill our stomach with excessive nervousness. Our sleep pattern is disturbed. We can't go to bed, and we cannot get up in the morning. In between, we toss and turn.

We feel tense, on edge, throughout the day. Often we can have a headache. Our eyes hurt. We cannot focus or pay attention. Our body has flu-like symptoms. Our joints ache. Everything is an effort. We prefer to do something physical rather than something spiritual. We avoid people and places where we may have to engage with them.

Emotionally, we are reactive. We do not listen properly. We are agitated, irritable, sad, and moody. We feel sorry for ourselves. We want sympathy, we don't want sympathy. We push people away. We drive people away. We are prone to being anxious, worried, fearful. We feign being unconcerned. We could care less what people think, but we are also worried about being rejected.

We are angry at everything. It simmers under the surface of all our interactions. We are on this roller coaster of feelings, yet we pretend there is nothing wrong. We can feel suspicious, mistrustful, and even cynical about people and situations.

Mentally, we question everything. We have this negative tape, background conversations, playing endlessly in our head. We speculate constantly; and most, if not all of it, is negative. We pick holes in what people say. We are hunting for game; and our mind is the rifle, and thoughts are the bullets.

We chase down everything and everyone that does not agree with us, and we shoot holes in them. We replay events negatively. We engage in mental conversations, movie scenes in our head, where we come out on top in the argument.

We vindicate ourselves or imagine others doing it for us. We believe the worst and look for it to happen. We become super-analytical. We pull fragments of thoughts together to form a negative picture that suits our feelings and the story we want to create.

When we are out of alignment, it is very difficult to trust anyone. We magnify the negatives to justify our wrong emotions. Every word and action is under a microscope. The enemy loves a poor mental state. He subtly adds more and more negativity until we are choked by it. We become suspicious of motives and people. We seek similar people to fellowship with in cynicism.

All these can become barriers where we form a resistance. We man the barricades to repel truth, wisdom, and the requirements of love. We prefer our own perceptions, no matter who they hurt. Spiritually, it leads to isolation. We come to a place of accusation. We ignore the Holy Spirit.

Sometimes non-alignment begins by something people can do or say that wounds us. An event can occur that can damage us. We lose self-control and allow ourselves to spiral down into the flesh. Usually, what happens is that anything in our hearts and lives that is not dealt with, now rises up to stake its claim on our lives.

In the aftermath of a negative circumstance or event, we initially feel contrary. If we have broken through these thoughts and feelings previously, they will not last now. It is a temporary reaction, and our usual spirituality will reassert itself. The place of the Holy Spirit in us will overcome. All we need generally is a place of quiet reflection.

If we have not broken through previously, what is rising up in us is our own carnality. Now we have a fight on our hands. The sad truth is that the vast majority of Christians are not under attack from the enemy but are actually being assaulted by their own carnality.

Why would the enemy waste time attacking people he already controls when instead he can use them to hurt or wound other people? Such people do not warrant an attack from the enemy; they do too good a number on themselves for him to waste his resources.

Negativity causes pressure and means we allow ourselves to be under attack from within. Inadequate alignment can lead to guilt, condemnation, unbelief, woundedness, and poor relationships.

Assignment

❋ Ask the Holy Spirit to run a diagnostic check on you physically, emotionally, mentally, and spiritually.

❋ Your chief requirement at this time is honesty and humility. Read 1 Corinthians 1:1-3 and Hebrews 5:12-14. Keep yourself in the love of God, and be merciful [Jude 1:21]. What fruit of the Spirit do you need to employ in your own heart?

❋ Write down your symptoms, and ask for help. Resist the stupid notion that you can do this yourself! (That would be the enemy speaking.)

Commission

* Be more conscious of the four states of health: physical, emotional, mental, and spiritual.
* Without being overbearing, look at your family and friends. Are there any signs of non-alignment with God?
* Write them down, pray over them. Think of the antidote.
* Important!! Read Galatians 6:1-2 before you speak to anyone.
* How will you say it? How can you help people around you to stay in alignment and not lose it?

Personal Notes

Evidence of True Alignment

In a word, alignment looks like *health*. A properly aligned spiritual warrior is rested for a fight. We are willing to be involved with God; we arrive early to the battle and leave late. We have physical commitment and energy to do something. We are willing to perform physical tasks to make it easier for people to engage God.

Warriors are emotionally stable, living within healthy stress levels. We practice being calm and considerate. We are peacemakers, trained to be joyful. Christians in alignment can see other people's perspectives on issues. This open-heartedness puts everyone around us at ease. Whether in good or bad situations, we move through life glorifying God. Alignment brings an emotional connection between the Holy Spirit and a spiritual warrior.

Mentally, a warrior becomes tuned into God's personality – thoughtful, considerate, kind, and concerned. We are able to present truth in love and mercy, even when it is difficult. We ignore the issue of *who* is right or wrong, and focus on *what* is right and wrong. The mind is free of enemy programming and is in constant interaction with God. Our mind and spirit are cooperating to release God's word in everything He wants us to do. In alignment, we have access to peace and wisdom.

When we choose to live in alignment, our spirit is always in the presence of God. It's as if we are always singing; worship flows out of us throughout the day. We live a life of gratefulness. We practice being thankful in every circumstance. Warriors love to have brilliant thoughts about God. Being God-conscious is an honor and a pleasure.

Everything comes together when we are in alignment – our body, soul, and spirit join forces and maintain our spiritual momentum. When we are aligned properly, we can move comfortably from the known to the unknown. We gain wisdom from every experience, and begin to learn how God thinks.

Alignment starts slowly, but we have to work our way through the gears to gain speed. But first gear is better than being stuck in reverse! It all starts with being faithful during the tests God has planted in our lives. When we take care of these little things, divine acceleration happens; and we move towards breakthrough.

Assignment

❀ Look at yourself positively. Imagine the Holy Spirit talking with you about your next upgrade.

❀ Looking at each of the four states of health: physical, emotional, mental and spiritual.

What do you feel He has planned for you in these areas in this season?

❄ What would you like to become in each of these areas in this next time period?

❄ Take time out to write your upgrade list.

Commission

❄ Apply your upgrade list to each area. Some of it will be an antidote to things you no longer need.

❄ Have fun replacing the negative with a positive alignment! Always enjoy the process.

❄ Look around you. Who else would benefit from a similar perspective?

Personal Notes

The Two Routes into Alignment

The Father uses two ways to develop us. They both take the same amount of time, energy and discipline. The route we take is always set by the Lord. We can ask Him for our preference, but He will choose the route that He believes is most beneficial for us at this time.

The first is an **impartation** that suddenly launches us into a whole new arena of favor and authority. For a season, things are wonderfully fluid and easy, eventually it slows down and moves us into **process,** where we will be tested on what the Father has given or become to us. Testing is vital for our development because it establishes our experience into truth that remains.

The truth now becomes values and principles that we live by continually as part of our relationship with the Holy Spirit.

The second route is a **process** that leads to divine acceleration. The Father begins to open up truth about life in Jesus. As He does so, the Holy Spirit begins to apply that truth to areas of our life. Process is about learning relational joy. All process is relational. In process, our Comforter is our tutor. We learn about the nature of God because He applies His heart to ours.

I adore process - the action of discovering God's nature for me and stepping into the truth of it.

Process is about obedience and choice. We learn obedience by what the Spirit takes us through in our circumstances. We make choices based on who God is for us and what He wants us to be.

Generally speaking, both routes work this way. Impartation works **from** experience into the truth. Process works with the truth **towards** a place of encounter. The impartation route works well with our emotions. We have an encounter with God that enables and empowers us to feel His Presence. We enter into a joyous experience that we enjoy absolutely. After a season of that, the process kicks in. Our emotions are sidelined. The feelings disappear, and now we have to learn to believe that God is still present. Process, then, is about thinking properly. It is about being renewed in the Spirit of your mind.

The impartation has given us the experience; now the process has to establish its reality when the feelings have disappeared. In warfare, the enemy attacks our emotions and our mindset. Both need to be strong. We need to receive under pressure, and this is fabulous training.

The process route works well with our thinking. *"As a man thinks in his heart, so is he." [Proverbs 23:7].* In process, the Holy Spirit develops our thinking so that we can choose to believe. Whatever God shows us, He gives us faith for that interaction. Process is about working with God on our issues and our lifestyle. It is transformational thinking

[Romans 12:2].

It is also about receiving promises and enjoying the Holy Spirit as He processes the truth into our hearts. The process route is about learning to think from our heart, not our head.

The natural man cannot understand the things of the Spirit of God. To his natural way of thinking, they seem foolish and hard to understand. They are not logical or rational, but spiritual; therefore, normal ways of reasoning do not apply [1 Corinthians 2:12-15].

When we do not live from our heart, then there is an absence of brightness in our thinking and perception. Our heart becomes dull. We are slow to learn and understand. We can lack clarity and sharpness in our thinking. Our spirituality becomes cloudy and dim. The effect on our life is that we become downcast and cheerless. When we see and hear from our heart, we understand what is happening and have every potential to be renewed [Matthew 13:14-15].

The whole point of process is to maintain our heart connection with the Father, in Jesus, by the Holy Spirit. As our heart increases, we develop our thinking and move towards accelerated input.

We practice obedience in our hearts [Romans 6:17]. The Word is in our heart, and our mouth confesses what our heart receives [Romans 10:8-10]. The Father has prepared many things for us which can only be seen and heard as we live in our heart, our inner self in the Spirit [1 Corinthians 2:9-10]. The person who stands firm in heart, has authority over his own will [1 Corinthians 7:37]. God writes on our hearts [2 Corinthians 3:3]; so that we can do His will from our inner man [Ephesians 6:5-6]. Our heart is always fully accessible to the processes of the Father [Hebrews 4:12]. It is our heart that empowers us to draw near in full assurance of faith [Hebrews 10:22], because it is confident when under the rule of the Spirit. It is the hidden person of the heart, with the imperishable quality of a gentle and quiet spirit, which is precious in the sight of God [1 Peter 3:4].

Divine acceleration comes to a heart that has engaged with process. We find ourselves being touched by God and coming into impartation and release. We can now have an experience of what the Lord has already established in the truth of our heart.

An impartation that does not lead to process means we do not get to keep the experience we have received. What is introduced by manifestation must be established in hiddenness. [*See *Hiddenness and Manifestation*, a journal from Brilliant Book house.com].

A process that does not result in impartation means that we have not encountered the Presence that increases the truth. Process that moves into impartation creates enlargement.

When someone becomes a spiritual warrior,

things open up. As we practice being in the presence of God, we are able to be taken into enemy territory without being harmed. He begins to trust us with the warfare that His presence provokes. He knows we will stay connected to Him and aligned with His purposes, even in difficult times.

Every believer is a soldier of Christ, but not everyone is a spiritual warrior. Warriors are on assignments specific to God's commands against the enemy. God wants to raise people who will live from the right motives and who can be trusted. He will not give this privilege to someone who has not passed His test. If we have not conquered the ground in our spirit, we will not be able to take anything from the enemy. It all starts with a choice within each of us -- do we trust God more than our own nature? The Father can only trust what He sees manifested of His Son within each of us.

Assignment

※ Have you recently had an impartation, a divine encounter with God? If you are still in it, then enjoy it!

※ If the feelings/sense of God's Presence has faded, do not try to recapture it. You cannot manufacture in your soul what the Holy Spirit has put into your inner man of the heart/spirit.

* You have now entered the process of learning to think from your heart. God is still present, but now you must believe the truth of it.
* What is the Father doing in your life that will upgrade His Presence in your character and lifestyle?
* Choose what needs an upgrade and get to work in your heart. **Remember** work from your place of encounter into the truth and the sense of His Presence will return.

Commission

* You are in process. Follow the teaching of the Spirit.
* Open up your heart to thinking, hearing, and seeing. Then you will understand everything.
* You are losing your grip on logic, reason, and rationale. You are not a cerebral believer -- you are a heart person enjoying the Holy Spirit.
* Enjoy the journey. As you learn something, take it into the place of praise, rejoicing, and thanksgiving.
* Intimacy establishes reality. Truth is best established in celebration.

＊ As you put time aside to celebrate what you are learning and becoming, then you are attracting the Presence of God to you. Encounter will surely come. Move towards it!

Personal Notes

Do Not Blur Your Focus

Spiritual warriors require outstanding focus. The enemy wants nothing more than to break our concentration on the things of God. He knows that basking in the light of God's nature grows us stronger every day, and the enemy wants to put a stop to it. We must focus on our God-given assignment, pouring our time, energy, finances, and attention into that goal. If the enemy can blur our focus, we become distracted, lose our vision, and are ultimately rendered insignificant.

Focus is vital to spiritual warfare and must be protected at all costs. It was so important in ancient Israel that God would not tolerate any distraction, as we read in Deuteronomy 13:6-10:

> *If your brother, the son of your mother, your son or your daughter, the wife of your bosom, or your friend who is as your own soul, secretly entices you, saying, 'Let us go and serve other gods,' which you have not known, neither you nor your fathers, of the gods of the people which are all around you, near to you or far off from you, from one end of the earth to the other end of the earth, you shall not consent to him or listen to him, nor shall your eye pity him, nor shall you spare him or conceal him; but you shall surely kill him; your hand shall be first against him to put him*

> *to death, and afterward the hand of all the*
> *people. And you shall stone him with stones*
> *until he dies, because he sought to entice you*
> *away from the LORD your God, who brought*
> *you out of the land of Egypt, from the house*
> *of bondage.*

This is an image of violent concentration. The penalty for allowing ourselves to be separated from God has always been death in every form. Sin separates. Idolatry puts people outside of a benevolent covenant. That was Israel's consistent testimony. They walked with God in righteousness, and He blessed them. They were seduced into sin and idol worship and went into bondage. They lost families, cities, regions, wars, and nations to sin and its consequences. They would cry out to God, repent and be restored, only for the cycle to begin again at a later date.

We are called to ignore things that would distract us from our God-given mandate, to put to death every distraction and to maintain focus as a way of life.

> *For those who live according to the flesh set*
> *their minds on the things of the flesh, but*
> *those who live according to the Spirit, the*
> *things of the Spirit. For to be carnally minded*
> *is death, but to be spiritually minded is life*
> *and peace. Because the carnal mind is enmity*
> *against God; for it is not subject to the law of*

God, nor indeed can be. So then, those who
are in the flesh cannot please God. But you
are not in the flesh but in the Spirit, if indeed
the Spirit of God dwells in you. Now if
anyone does not have the Spirit of Christ, he
is not His. [Romans 8:5-9].

Distraction kills passion. We are focused or unfocused. Focus occurs when our mind is set, centered, fixed on a certain goal. It's hard to love someone without being consistent. It is impossible to please someone when our relationship is unclear and indistinct. We actually set up a scenario where hostility develops rather than passion. Relationships become incompatible when love has lost its focus.

Jesus, in Matthew 5:29-30, gives us an updated version of this Deuteronomy 13 principle –

If your right eye causes you to sin, pluck it out
and cast it from you; for it is more profitable
for you that one of your members perish, than
for your whole body to be cast into hell. And
if your right hand causes you to sin, cut it off
and cast it from you; for it is more profitable
for you that one of your members perish, than
for your whole body to be cast into hell.

Lack of focus is a major handicap, like losing an eye or a hand. It makes life much more difficult. We can have a life without focus, but it will be one of stunning mediocrity. Ask yourself: "What have I really achieved in the last 1-3 years?" Write a list of your accomplishments.

Now ask yourself: "With all the time I had at my disposal, what could I have achieved with more focus?" The difference between the two details your current disposition.

We need to get rid of the things that distract us. Jesus continually encouraged His disciples to focus on the Kingdom of God. Everything he taught them was to focus them on the Kingdom. *"But seek first the kingdom of God and His righteousness, and all these things shall be added to you,"* Jesus said in Matthew 6:33. If we try anything without possessing this focus, we will be unsuccessful and ultimately frustrated.

Failure occurs because of weak and inaccurate focus. Sometimes we do too much, and it decreases our focus. Jesus Himself went away to pray to maintain His own focus; He had to get past people and issues and find a quiet place with God. Often the enemy will use overload and overwork to fracture our focus. We can quickly end up being more engaged in ministry than in fellowship with God. If our ministry is outweighing our time with the Lord, we are in serious trouble. This is one of the hurdles that Martha could not overcome in Luke 10:38-42:

> *Now it happened as they went that He entered a certain village; and a certain woman named Martha welcomed Him into her house. And she had a sister called Mary, who also sat*

at Jesus feet and heard His word. But Martha
was distracted with much serving, and she
approached Him and said, "Lord, do You not
care that my sister has left me to serve alone?
Therefore tell her to help me."

And Jesus answered and said to her, "Martha,
Martha, you are worried and troubled about
many things. But one thing is needed, and
Mary has chosen that good part, which will
not be taken away from her."

Under normal circumstances, Martha was
right; Mary should have been helping her. But this
was not a normal houseguest. This was Jesus, which
meant Martha was wrong in this instance. Jesus used
the opportunity to teach Martha about focus and how
it makes us truly spiritual. He wants all of us, not a
part of us.

Similarly, a job or career that makes us too
tired to live, is killing us, and quite possibly, the
relationships around us. Within the framework of
loving, caring relationships we must have passionate
focus. Otherwise, we abandon people by default.
Sometimes passion is about extremes of how we love
and bless people. It requires the constant flow of
being faithful in small ways, plus the occasions where
we push the boat out and go for the max.

Too many small things only, makes love
ordinary. Only doing the big, grand gesture makes

love unpredictable and inconsistent. Both together keep it special.

When we say "yes" to Jesus we must say "no" elsewhere or our focus becomes blurred. *"Let your yes be yes, and your no, be no."* If our yes to one thing is not followed by a no elsewhere, we will lose focus at some point. Focus provides engagement. When a woman says yes to a man's proposal of marriage, all other men cease to exist on a romantic level. Her heart is fixed. If she is still looking around, then either the guy is not the right one or she needs some life counseling!

If an athlete wants to compete in the Olympics, there needs to be a "no" to any activity that works against his fitness and preparation.

I am a lover of God and a worshipper who adores meditation as a way of life. I am a husband, father, grandfather, brother, and best friend. I am a speaker, author, leader, consultant, project adviser, and businessman. I love my friends, reading, soccer, parties, movies, walking, good conversation, and shopping for my wife. I travel more than I would like. I am developing my own training center. I love to help my family and friends succeed. I am an investor in people and projects like anti-human trafficking. I have a strong focus on helping my friends and family go to the next level of their identity.

I believe in strategic life exchange and love to spend time with the people I love, thinking about who they are becoming and contemplating their next step of faith. I love to invest time, energy, love, and money in the relationships around me.

Believing the best about someone is fabulous. Helping them to become bigger in God and better at their identity is a joyful part of my life with them.

We have a destiny together, and I am jealous for them to do well and have a great life.

Because I am focused on my family and friends, I can help them focus.

I am fully engaged in a life I love, and I know how to be at rest, relaxed, and live in a celebratory fashion. Time, not money, is the currency of my life; I work with God to redeem time.

> *See then that you walk circumspectly, not as fools but as wise, redeeming the time, because the days are evil.*
> *Therefore do not be unwise, but understand what the will of the Lord is. [Ephesians 5:15-17].*

Making the most of time available is critical if we are to become renowned in the Kingdom. Great people make time; good people find time; mediocre people waste time. Some people's use of time borders on the criminal. It is a resource more important than money. Saying "no" so that our "yes" becomes more significant, is vital to our lifestyle.

Focus determines our level of power and influence. Whatever has the capacity to keep our attention has influence over us. Focus directs our energy. When our heart is focused on God, we develop stamina as we are occupied with Him.

There is one cast iron certainty about people that will always be true. Given the choice, they will always do exactly what they want to do. Whenever people bleat that they have no time for something, it is usually that they have no passion for it, or they need to say "no" elsewhere.

Every day is a blessing from God. Our focus determines our energy level for that day. Imagine you are at home on your couch, feeling sleepy, and watching TV. Suddenly the telephone rings, and you are told that a family member has been rushed to the hospital. Do you go back to the couch and your state of malaise? Of course not! You have been instantly focused on what is important – the health of your loved one. You grab your coat, jump in the car, and speed off to the hospital. Your focus has given you energy.

Our focus gives us the power to pursue something long term. It helps us plan and strategize. I love being led by the Holy Spirit, but I do have a five-year plan. I have a compass that points me in the direction I need to travel. Not everything is set in stone, but I know the direction I am headed. I have focus.

A vision without a plan is just wishful thinking. In Philippians 3:14-15, Paul clearly states that he has a focus for his life –

> *Brethren, I do not count myself to have apprehended; but one thing I do, forgetting those things which are behind and reaching forward to those things which are ahead, I press toward the goal for the prize of the upward call of God in Christ Jesus.*

Paul was not a prisoner of his past; he had made it a point to be free of everything that might jeopardize his focus.

A broken focus will destroy our dreams. To stay aligned with what God is doing, we have to sometimes make tough choices. James knew how important focus was – *"But let him ask in faith, with no doubting, for he who doubts is like a wave of the sea driven and tossed by the wind,"* he wrote in James 1:6-8. *"For let not that man suppose that he will receive anything from the Lord; he is a double-minded man, unstable in all his ways."* Double mindedness cannot be an option – we need a singular focus; otherwise we will waver at a critical moment.

Spiritual warriors cannot receive anything from God if we are unfocused. By aligning ourselves with God, we develop the ability to receive from Him. Remember His charge to Joshua in Joshua 1:7-8:

> *Only be strong and very courageous, that you may observe to do according to all the law*

which Moses My servant commanded you; do not turn from it to the right hand or to the left, that you may prosper wherever you go. This Book of the Law shall not depart from your mouth, but you shall meditate in it day and night, that you may observe to do according to all that is written in it. For then you will make your way prosperous, and then you will have good success.

Success will only come when a spiritual warrior is focused. Faith requires focus. Without faith it is impossible to please God. A vision gives us focus. A blurred vision handicaps us in life. A blurred focus handicaps our spirituality and makes us less effective in the Kingdom.

Assignment

❊ What are the areas where you lack focus or have become stalled in your life?

❊ What must you do to get your relationship with God back on track at a higher level?

❊ Describe your passions and what they mean to you.

❊ Are there any specific areas where you are double minded or not fully engaged?

❊ Write a concise vision statement for each broken focus.

Commission

❋ What is your focus in the relationships that God has put around you? What do you get to be for those people consistently?

❋ How can you help them receive an upgrade and be successful in the present?

Personal Notes

Developing Consistency

There is no such thing as a quick fix or a magic formula. It takes real commitment to create a positive transformation. The majority of people attending conferences around the world see no improvement in their lives. Some of that is because the content of ministry is poor. Mostly though, people do not take time to implement what they learn.

Good discipleship will lay proper foundations for focus and commitment and then build on it by handling specific issues. The reason most people fail in their focus is because they are used to passivity and procrastination.

The enemy loves docile believers. They are compliant, never a threat, mostly resigned, and easily persuaded to inactivity. Majesty breaks passivity because it opens people up to all the claims of sovereignty. When we understand and receive God's supremacy as a fact, then our experience produces assertiveness. Faith is active; unbelief is passive. If we are not engaged, we do not believe.

Life is about choices and how we respond to situations. Bad choices promote disaster; good choices increase our blessing and favor. Our everyday preferences determine abundance or poverty. Good, consistent choices lay the foundations for good habits to emerge that will enhance our long term future.

A consistent lifestyle is founded on values and principles that guide our internal and external behaviors. It is important that we identify how habits really work, both for and against us. Check out unproductive habits, and develop a framework to produce successful practices. Focus on what works, not what doesn't.

A habit is something that we do so often that it becomes easy! It is a behavior that we keep repeating until it becomes automatic, like driving a car. At the outset, we wonder if we will ever master everything without killing someone. A few years later, the practice is so ingrained it has become second nature.

The Holy Spirit is astonishing in His ability to empower us to do the opposite to what ails us. Empowerment is a choice. So is disempowerment. We all have beliefs about ourselves that need to change:

"I'm not good at prayer." "I don't feel God ever." "I am not creative." "God will not meet me." "I can't speak publicly." "I'm too nervous, too fearful." "I could never do that." "I'm not worthy of being loved."

Disempowerment is always concerned with our perceived or actual performance. Some people can't see themselves doing something, so they don't try. Other people fail, but don't learn.

Empowerment is rooted in God's nature. *"I can do all things in Christ who strengthens [empowers] me." [Philippians 4:13].* If we build our devotional time on who God is in Himself and on who He wants to be for us, then His strength comes into our weakness automatically. We are fully empowered by focusing on who He is for us. He consistently empowers us to become. As we behold Him, we become like Him.

The Holy Spirit is fabulous at reframing our thoughts and reprogramming our behaviors. In reframing, He adjusts our perceptions and thoughts about ourselves, life, and circumstances. When our language is adjusted, we think better. At a dinner party a few years ago, I sat across the table from a woman that I had not met before. She began to tell me about the dream job she had just landed at a company she had always wanted to work for.

Her conversation was dominated by several negative comments about herself. She doubted her ability to compete in this new environment, her capacity to do the job effectively, her experience in management, and her technical prowess in using different products. Her final comment was, "I'm really fearful of starting work there."

I looked at her and said, "But what if you're not fearful; what if you're just apprehensive?" I went on to explain that such a high-powered company would not employ under-powered people.

Her perception of herself was disempowering her. God had given her a dream job and was therefore engaged in empowering her to do it! Whose report would she believe?

It's a version of the Canaan spy syndrome. Twelve special forces guys were sent out; only two came back. The other ten went out as warriors and returned as wimps [Numbers chapter 13]. They were so intimidated by what they saw that their perception of themselves was, *"We became like grasshoppers in our own sight." [v 33].*

Joshua and Caleb went out with a sense of God's majesty and what they saw only increased it! The main issue of our life should always be to please the Lord. "If He is pleased with us, He will give it to us. Do not rebel against the Lord; these people will be our prey. Their protection has been removed and God is with us" [14:7-9].

God had given this woman her dream job as an empowerment, and she was talking herself out of His provision. It's normal to be apprehensive in a new and unknown situation. The Father, however, is a known quantity who fits in the gap between her current experience and her new learning curve!

"What if the Father is excited about all that He gets to be for you in this new season? Your dream job needs a dream upgrade in your relationship with Him. What does that look like?" As we talked, her posture changed. Her eyes became bright, her voice animated. We were talking about the Father's goodness and all the possibilities it would generate.

She began to be excited at what the Father had planned for her. "What if you're not apprehensive, but quietly apprehensive and mostly excited?" I asked.

We talked about the genius of the Holy Spirit and His cheerful exuberance. She smiled and laughed. I told her some stories of what the Holy Spirit is like and how wonderful it is to rely on Him.

Her face shone. "I can't wait to start work and believe God," she said.

"What if you're not quietly apprehensive, but faintly nervous and mostly intrigued by what God will be for you?" I asked. Her eyes twinkled. "Ok, I get it!! The One who gave me the job will empower me to do the job!"

Exactly. That is reframing - subtly altering the picture by using a series of frames to create a new image. As our thoughts become reframed, our behavior can become reprogrammed.

From an anxious, intimidated posture we can become excited and purposeful about depending on the Lord. With a different attitude comes a different approach. The adjustments we make become new habits as the Holy Spirit empowers and enlightens our hearts and lives. We get to keep our breakthroughs and establish ourselves in the goodness and kindness of God. We become consistent with who God is for us.

"We make no provision for the flesh."
[Romans 13:14] which can also mean that we do not make allowances for failure or negativity. Failure becomes good as we learn, and horrible if we do not.

Passivity and procrastination are habits of the flesh. We are dabbling at life rather than being engaged with it. Habits determine our quality of life and/or future destiny. Our identity must be firmly established in that we are in Christ, learning to be Christ-like. Successful people do not drift to the top. It takes focus, discipline, and energy - all of which the Lord Jesus has in abundance!

A warrior knows that it is our inner life that is the key to consistency. Learning to be faithful in our small adjustments will empower us to make big changes over a prescribed period. That is what times and seasons are in the Spirit. They are prescribed periods of promise and provision that lead to breakthrough, upgrade, and promotion. In that prescribed period, we have the pleasure of being reframed and reprogrammed in the Spirit - made more Christ-like.

In this prescribed period, take time to adjust perception. Warriors will take time to explore and expand their permission and increase their awareness of God.

Whatever we do in a certain way will give us a predictable result - good or bad. The Holy Spirit redeems our routines so that we become accustomed to life at a new level.

When I see certain behaviors (good or poor), my question is the same: "What is it that this person is believing about themselves that makes them behave in this way?" If it's a good behavior, I like to encourage and empower the person in what I see and appreciate about them. If it's a poor behavior, I want to encourage and empower them to see themselves differently. Reshaping personal beliefs is a key discipling tool.

When stress levels rise, people can slip back into old habit patterns. Developing internal rest has been a huge part of my journey. When time, energy, and effort are at a low, we are in stress. Personal rest will enable us to focus on the Holy Spirit so that we can abide in Christ despite circumstances.

More than three quarters of our normal behavior is based on an acquired habit. Our outward behavior is the truth. Our inward perception of our behavior is often an illusion.

Our environment can shape our belief systems and our habits. Warriors are making choices about who they hang out with and are therefore influencing their behavior. People do not have to be bad to influence us negatively. Just having no focus or passion will create a climate of mediocrity. If we hang out with a bunch of drifters, we will drift.

Negative environments will produce: low self esteem, fear, unworthiness, lack of confidence, passivity, procrastination, deception, lack of passion, no vision, and cover up.

A positive environment creates: warmth, energy, supportive relationships, truth, belief, confident expectation, opportunities, a sense of adventure, and willingness to take risks.

The beauty of the Holy Spirit is that He is totally committed to our development. There is always another level to go to! Warriors are rightly concerned with the long term consequences of unproductive habits.

In my home church, The Mission, as we were going through a transitional period we made some key decisions that would define who we wanted to be as a community of believers. It was a huge turning point for us as a company of like-minded people.

[The book <u>Decisions That Define Us</u> by David Crone, Mission team leader, is available at Brilliantbookhouse.com].

Usually, our new habit is either the opposite of the one that is not working or an upgrade on one that is doing OK. Start with the benefits and rewards of going to a new level. Create a clear picture of what developing a new/better habit will do for you.

It is best to work towards something rather than away from something. For Israel, getting away from Egypt was clearly their priority rather than moving into Canaan.

Closure is not enough by itself. We must be converted to new habits and behaviors. A rabble of slaves must be connected to a disciplined army that could take territory. Israel never adjusted because they did not understand the conversion process that would develop them into warriors who could receive their inheritance.

Their habits did not change; they lost focus, and were incapable of possessing the identity required to enter the fight. After the conversion process has achieved its aims, we can be commissioned to enter into our inheritance. Commission produces authority that arises out of an upgraded identity.

Warriors are focused people, centered on Christ and fully alive in the Holy Spirit. They are persistent, consistent, and undeviating in their approach to the Father. They are accustomed to fighting and overcoming. They have a passionate disposition and established routines that bless the Lord. They are clear thinkers with distinctive actions that define their spirituality. They are consecrated and concentrated.

Assignment

❊ What are your unproductive habits?

* Identify your bad habits and ask for feedback from family and friends.
* How has the enemy rendered you docile, compliant, resigned to life, and resistant of change?
* How will you and the Holy Spirit counter that and develop new routines?

Commission

* What is the Holy Spirit empowering in you?
* What is your current prescribed period of adjustment?
* Who do you want to be, regardless of circumstances?
* What do you want to become, regardless of the pressures?

Read Decisions that Define Us and make your own list of decisions that will define the quality of life you want to cultivate.

Personal Notes

Releasing the Warrior!...A Prophecy

Read this word silently four times.

Firstly, read it through normally. Catch the cadence of it. Allow pictures to form in your heart. See yourself as a warrior. Hear God's voice to your heart.

Secondly, read it through peacefully. Come to as much peace as you are able and read it slowly, gently, from within your heart. Let the simple power of God's intention for you gently overwhelm all your senses. Then relax and think calmly about all the images that He brings into your conscious mind.

Thirdly, read it through with joy. Let the majesty of God wash over you. Relax in His sovereign power. The victory is yours; the battle is the Lord's. Warriors are happy people who celebrate God's supremacy. Feel His joy rise up in you.

Fourthly, read it with strength. Imagine yourself prophesying this word over a company of people before a fight. Say it with strength so that power flows into them. Feel the strength of it yourself!

NOW DO THE WHOLE EXERCISE AGAIN, OUT LOUD! Read it through four times with a clear voice. Walk around, reading it.

Stand your ground, and read it aloud - like a Herald. Be seated in Christ, and read it with His voice. Each time you read it, open your heart to becoming a warrior. Let the desire of it rise up within you. Receive it! Let it flow into you and fill you. Let your heart move into majesty. Rejoice in the strength and power of Almighty God.

Allow all the tensions and stress to disappear. Let your heart be touched. When you read it aloud, listen with your heart. **REALLY** listen with your heart. Allow the love and enthusiasm of God to overwhelm you.

Work it in!

When you have read it all through several times, read each part, study it, think about it. **Importantly.** Imagine yourself in it. Answer the questions and do the assignments, using the space provided.

Please note:
There is a CD version of this prophetic word available from Brilliantbookhouse.com. It can be obtained in two ways:
1. Buy the conference teaching series: "Way of the Warrior" for $46.00 including shipping. The prophecy CD is included.

2. Buy the Prophetic Soaking CD: *"Rise up a Warrior"* separately for $12 including shipping.

Part 1.....RISE UP ... A WARRIOR

My beloved, this is a time of New Beginnings.
I am promoting you in the Spirit.
I am drawing you up to a new place of ENCOUNTER.

As a foot soldier, you have fought well.
You have tasted the sweetness of victory and the
ashes of defeat.
You have learned to persevere.
You have embraced a steadfast and faithful lifestyle.

You have learned to stand and press in.
You understand the importance of remaining fresh.
You are able to refuse weariness.
You have overcome the spirit of heaviness
that was against you on this level.

Now, I AM ... is calling you up to a new place of
overcoming.
I am calling you to walk the Way of the Warrior.
To rise up into a place of Abundance and Provision
that will provide you with rich encounters with Me
on the battlefields of life.

In this season of preparation and re-arming
you must leave the last remains of mediocrity behind.
Where I AM ... is taking you ... you cannot have a
smallness of mind.
Indeed you must renew your mind just to enter this
new place.

This new season is about you stepping away
out of your circumstances into a new place in Christ.
You do not live in your circumstances, you live in
Me.
Now you must discover the awesome permission that
means for you ... in My intention.

You must see Me as I really am.
Not as your church experience depicts me.
You must be upgraded in every way.
I will show you the God of the Heavens
and you will walk in the God of the Kingdom.

Assignment

⁂ In your current situation you have permission
to overcome everything that is against you.
⁂ What have you learned; or still need to learn
about • perseverance • pressing in •
remaining fresh • refusing weariness?

❋ Describe the areas of mediocrity that you want to eradicate. BE HONEST.

When learning to be an overcomer, we discover that we are the ones that need to be overcome!

Commission

❋ What does your current smallness of mind look like? What do you need the Holy Spirit to do in you to upgrade your thinking?

❋ Describe what stepping out of your circumstances and into Christ would look and feel like for you.

Personal Notes

Part 2.....A New Dimension

I AM ... is calling you to a new dimension
of the power and place of the Spirit.
Where Truth is the gateway to experience
and encounters with Me release the wisdom of My
ways.

I am calling you to walk in the power of My
perception about you.
For your life to be governed by how I see you.
For you to embrace My identity for you.
That you would live in the Majesty of My Affection.
Undaunted, unworried, unbeatable.

My perception of you, will upgrade your D.N.A. in
the Spirit.
No longer a child ... but a son ... moving into
maturity.
Learning your authority.
Embracing your liberty.

The D.N.A. of Sonship gives you access to different
dimensions of permission, inheritance and authority.
From this place you will have a deeper, broader
authorization over the enemy.

Foot soldiers are empowered. Warriors are embraced
… in power and permission.
Sonship elevates you to inhabit, not just visit, the
place of My Abundance.

In this place you will discover your **true** self.
As you develop the obedience to live within My
intentionality,
you will learn to live in harmony with My delight in
you.
This unity with the Spirit will be the source of your
overcoming lifestyle in this next dimension.

I will teach you how to make the future incredible by
living in a present that is beautiful.
When the present state of your heart is so enriched
by My glory,
your current identity will run to meet your emerging
destiny.
And you will live in the power of an Accelerated
Lifestyle.

Do you see now … Dear Heart … why you need the
power of a renewed mind?
Earthbound logic cannot comprehend the true nature
of life in the Spirit.
Only a heavenly mindset can do that. The mind of
Christ.

Assignment

※ If there was one verse or passage of scripture that would be a gateway for you to enter into a new dimension…what would it be?
Ask the Holy Spirit for one!

※ Explain what this scripture means to you and how you will use it to enter your permissions.
[*Isaiah 41:8-16 was the author's gateway promise that has sustained him for many years. He still reads it and meditates on it, today].

Commission

※ What would it take for you to learn to live in the majesty of God's affection?

※ Describe your D.N.A. in Christ and what must change in your to establish that reality.

Personal Notes

Part 3...Create an Internal Environment

Beloved, environment is critical to development.
It is time for you to rise up and occupy a new place in
the Spirit.
When you rest in My affection. what can you
imagine?
Allow My Spirit to stir up your heart to think in a
new way.

I will enlighten the inner man of your heart.
My words shall rise from your inner man
into your natural mind, so that it is renewed, in the
fullness of Christ.
When your conscious mind comes under the spirit of
Wisdom and revelation in the inner man ...
... you shall see clearly and know definitely your
emerging identity.

Beloved, I charge you therefore ... do not be
earthbound in your thinking.
Intellectuals do not have empowered perception in
the Spirit.
They merely have enlarged insight within the realm
of logic and reason.
It is perception from a smaller place of being.

You must see in the Spirit. Enlightenment begins with a vision of something, or Someone that causes an increase of faith and vitality.

Your emerging identity has a vitality and a beauty that is irresistible to Me.

It's My bride emerging.

She lives in such deep affection in My heart, and that shapes her personality and identity.

She has all the permissions of love bestowed on her.

My intentions are My permissions!!

Call yourself up to a new place of permission granted.

In this new persona, everyone around you will be influenced by My passion for you.

As My warrior princess, you will live as you **should** in Me, before men.

People will be confronted by My Majesty when they see you living as the Beloved.

It will do wonders for the souls of people around you.

The life in you will not allow people to live a reduced lifestyle.

Your confidence in Me will overpower their doubts.

And though, initially ... antagonized by your confession,

They shall receive an upgrade in My Presence.

Everything you touch will increase.

Everyone that you speak to, will rise up -
If not initially … always eventually.
Stay true to the new you!

Live in harmony with My delight in you, and your
desires will form a deeper place of permission for
others.
There are many levels of blessing and inheritance.
They are linked to your response and fellowship with
Me.
Walk with Me into this place of favor which will
always be as deep as you wish it to be.
I am always ready to bless you.
My heart is always fully towards you.

I want you to live in the place of unbroken delight
Where the poverty of sin cannot touch you.
Where My newness of life embraces you everyday.
Where My favor renews you in the Spirit each
morning.
And you live … empowered by joy … under the
beauty of My smile.

Assignment

✳ There is a Secret Place on the inside of you, in
your heart, where God dwells with you and
where you abide in Him. Read John 15:1-11.
What does abiding mean to you?

* Describe the inner man and the importance of living from within.
* In what ways are you earthbound in your thinking? Why are logic and reason no help in thinking from the Spirit?

Commission

* For men – What does it mean to think and see as a Bride?
* For women – What does it mean to think and see as a Bride?
* For both – What does a warrior princess do and how does she interact with Jesus?
* Describe the impact and effect such a relationship would have on the lives of others.

Personal Notes

Part 4....New Depths of Habitation

Behold, I make My face shine upon you.
I am delighted in you … remain there.
Abide in My Keeping Power.
Dwell in the place of fullness … which is perpetual
blessing.
My grace overwhelms everything you are not
so that I may fully gaze on you, My beloved, My
beauty.
And your heart shall melt with delight and favor
as you walk in the peace and blessing of your God.

I have brought you to a deeper place of favor and
inheritance.
A deep well of provision is **inside** you!
A deep river of blessing is **before** you.
The first opens up the second. Your internal focus is
the key to external freedom.

To drink deep is an act of worship.
There is a new depth available. Go to a deeper place
of delight.

When I open you up to new depths of My love,
it will expose the hidden things in you, that prevent
you
from fully experiencing Me.
My goodness eradicates despair.

My mercy illuminates self-hatred.
My joy exposes low self-esteem.

I am not exposing you to ridicule, Beloved, but to
Acceptance and Wholeness.
I am exposing you to your own greatness in Me.

A fresh revelation of My nature upgrades you to
stand in a new dimension in the Spirit.
In this place I have set a fresh provision before you, to
bring you to
a higher place than you have risen to.
Come up higher, Beloved. Hear Me continuously
whisper to you …
"Arise, arise My love. My fair one."

The call upon you is to rise up, occupy a higher,
deeper, broader place in My name and My Nature.
To learn to **inhabit** this dimension, not just visit it.
The time of visitation is over.
The place of habitation has been erected.
You are in it and surrounded by it.
A place higher than the enemy can affect … has been
created for you.
Rise up and inhabit. Enter a high place of My
affection.

Come in!! Enter a new environment of faith and
permission.

The door is open.

You are in a new season. You have a new beginning. Do not look about you and say: "But, I'm still in the old place!"

You are in a new beginning. It has already occurred. You receive it first in Spirit ... then it becomes the truth in your experience.

You are in! Learn the lessons of abiding.

Remain here. Dwell here. Stay here!!

Explore this higher place.

Allow Me to give you a new vision for life in the Spirit.

When you have a fresh perspective, you can see more.

Assignment

❋ Look at your situations closely. What would fullness mean for you in each of them? What would it look like?

❋ What provision and blessing are available and permissible for you in Christ for each of your circumstances?

Commission

❋ What does the nature of God look like in the low places of your life and experience?

❄ When you consider the beauty of His nature and goodness, what provisions can you imagine?

❄ You are already in a place of habitation. Describe how you would stay and dwell there?

❄ What partnership is required with the Holy Spirit in order to have a habitation and not a visitation experience?

Personal Notes

Part 5....Overcoming a Poverty Spirit

I am removing a poverty spirit from your heart.
A poverty spirit keeps you trapped in a lower form of being.
Poverty is not about economic deficiency.
True poverty is the acceptance of meager possibility.

There can be a poverty of imagination.
A deficiency in courage. A death in personal vision.
A barrenness in the will that keeps you passive and beaten down.
Poverty is accepting a limitation and being governed by lack.

My people convince themselves that they lack resources, but the reality is,
they do not go out to meet My provision.
They take no steps of faith, they wait for provision to come.

I have placed provision, not where you stand,
but in the place you are **about** to tread.
It's in front of you, Beloved, one step ahead of a poverty mindset.

Never let yourself be defined by externals … your bank balance,
your resources, your environment.
Be defined internally by My permission.
Then, such as you have … I will always multiply.

I want you to re-think your assumptions about what is or is not possible …
in the light of your favor, and your faith in My intentionality.
Your personal assumptions will either defeat you or inspire you to live in Me.

Take ground in My permission.
Enter into agreement with My intention.
Internal harmony with My purpose is the basis for all warfare to succeed.
Contend with the enemy using your promises.
Believers are not passive … they apprehend!!

Your promises sharpen your courage in the battle.
Warfare must always reveal your inheritance.
It opens up new territory or establishes your present claim
because I AM territorial, so is My word.
Your promise has territory attached to it.
That is why the enemy contends against it.

In order to defeat you, he must prevent you from inheriting.
To do that, he must cast doubts on the promise you hold.
My people are a shadow of their potential, because they believe a lie.
The promise is designed to release you from fear into joy.

Fear is always present in a fight.
It has to be somewhere.
When you live above fear, it becomes a weapon in your hand,
and you drive it into the heart of the enemy.

Do not for a moment be intimated by the enemy,
for it is a sure sign to him, and to you,
that you are not believing in your promises.
Doubt attracts attack. The enemy seeks to do more than depress you.
He seeks you for an ally.
Warriors cannot be turned. Their heart is fixed on Me.

Warriors live in the laughter of their King.
They inhabit a place of carefree joy.
They walk in the exuberance and enthusiasm of the Holy Spirit.
They hear Me singing, and they learn the words.
They hear Me singing the Songs of Deliverance, and they join in.

All warriors are singers. The song of the Lord is glorious, and it is dangerous to all our foes.

Assignment

❊ When you think of a poverty spirit, what does that phrase mean to you?
❊ Where has your life been blighted by poverty thinking, and how will you correct that with the help of the Holy Spirit?
❊ Examine the problem areas of your life currently. Where has the Father placed your provision, and how will you step into it with His support?

Commission

❊ How would you rethink your assumptions more positively?
❊ The Father is being extremely intentional with your life. What agreements should you

make and keep in line with His desires for you?

❋ Promises are available…ask! How would you use God's promise as a weapon of war?

❋ What is the place of laughter that the Father has set aside for you?

Personal Notes

Part 6….. The Rights of an Overcomer

Come up higher. Occupy a higher place in My
affection.
A higher place of sensitivity in the Spirit is awaiting
you.
This is My promise to you:
"The place in your life where you have been counted
out
will become the place of your greatest encounter in
Me."

These difficulties will now tell you a different story.
It is the story of your present and future overcoming.
Behold, I grant you the rights of an overcomer in all
your
current areas of difficulty.
A higher place with Me guarantees a broader scope of
victory.

The enemy will now reveal to you the hand of God
upon you.
Watch closely from your high place.
For this purpose have I raised up the enemy, that I
may demonstrate My power over Him, in you.
All warriors know this and participate in My purpose.

There is always revelation in the battle -
A higher purpose than the fight itself.

When the enemy comes in like a flood,
I am always lifting up a standard against him.

That standard is My Name and My Nature ... in you.
On the battlefield there is fresh revelation of who you
are becoming -
An identity for you to step into.
I have placed both an increase and an upgrade on the
battlefield.
David knew that. It was why he ran towards Goliath.
It was that attitude that made him a man after My
own heart.

The current difficulties will define for you a new
place of identity.
Rise up and occupy a new persona in My Presence.
This is the year of your rising.
I am calling you up to a high place in My loving-
kindness and favor.
Be sheltered by My grace over you. Be protected in
My love.
Be cloaked in My power.
Stand above the enemy. Rise up ... above the
difficulty.

I always play to win.
For you to overcome, you must face the battle in the
same way that I do.
You fight from victory, not towards it.

Therefore, every battle is not yours to win.
It has already been won.
The battle is yours to lose, Beloved.
As you stand in Me, winning is your only option.

Because of these Truths, you must understand that I
send you out as a lamb against wolves.
In the natural, it will always look like you are
overwhelmed.
But you stand in the shadow of the Almighty.
You must have something big to overcome so that
you may grow
bigger by what you defeat.

Recognize the giant that is against you.
Expect to be lifted up above the head of your enemy.
The enemy **exists** to make **you** bigger!

When I lift you above him … you are thrusting down
at him …
as though you were on horseback and he on foot.
You have a Divine Advantage. I will teach you to use
it well.
You have favor with Me because I AM biased toward
you.

You are in a new season, a new beginning.
I am raising up the modern day equivalent of David's mighty men -
People who are after My own heart. Men and women of a different spirit ...
A people greatly Beloved, who understand their favor, and have
confidence in their own identity in Me.

There is therefore, Beloved, a season of preparation and training that I want to commit you to, on this next phase of your journey.
All the circumstances of your life I will use to train and equip you for this next dimension of the Spirit, that I wish to thrust you into.

Once you say "yes" to this development, there is no turning back; the training will begin.
I want you to live an ascended lifestyle, where you process your life **from** heaven to earth.
That is, you live by every word that proceeds from My mouth.
You take your perceptions of reality from the Holy Spirit and not from your own logic and reason.
I will teach you a higher level of perception and thinking -
One that will lead you into greater faith, and a more overtly outrageous, supernatural lifestyle.

Assignment

❋ You are granted the rights of an overcomer in all your current areas of difficulty. What encounters with God are now possible?

❋ What revelations are being bestowed upon you as the Father releases your warrior spirit?

❋ Name the identity that the Father is revealing to you at this time. Give it a title and describe its qualities!

Commission

❋ What does it mean to fight from victory not towards it? Explain.

❋ What is your Divine Advantage, and how will you use it?

❋ What does it mean to be a man/woman of a different spirit?

❋ Imagine living your life as the Beloved. What would it look and feel like?

Personal Notes

Part 7.....This is How it Works:

The faster you move, the more you will encounter,
and the more you will be transformed.
I am calling you to an Ascended lifestyle,
to learn the disciplines of a Resurrected Life.

I will teach you how to rejoice in the throne room.
You shall be enthusiastically immersed in throne
room praise.
I will develop your intercession before the throne...
You will take part in prophetic dialogue concerning
the nations, as Isaiah did.
And you will learn to pray with Jesus.

You will discover practical ways of being seated with
Christ in heavenly places.
You shall enter a deep place of rest.

You will develop and learn the joy of authority over
the enemy.
You will cultivate in My Presence, a divine military
intelligence over the enemy, as Elisha learned in his
day.

Above all, you shall be clothed in My Majesty.
For you will embrace My identity as your own.
Your revelation shall lead you into powerful
experiences that will transform your life.

Beloved, these disciplines will take time.
I am calling you to set time aside for Majesty to develop.

It is vital that your heart is overwhelmed by love.
For this season will be most joyful, and very painful for you.

The pain will come because you will have to leave behind lessons you have been taught, which you will discover, were not real truths about Me.
You will have to set aside logic and reason, in favor of wisdom and intuition.
You will discover that knowledge and experience were not what you imagined.

I will confront in you all religious teaching that does not represent Who I AM.
You must be free indeed, if you are to be a true warrior.

To counteract the pain, I will immerse you in My joy.
I will baptize you in freshness.
Your life will become new everyday.
You **must** practice renewal constantly ... or you will let it go in the heat of battle.

Beloved, do not be worried about this process of renewal.

Instead, be as excited for yourself as I am for you.

I will squeeze you through a narrow place so that your mind and heart become radically changed.

It will hurt only for a necessary season, but My joy in you shall always be present.

Come on this journey with Me, Beloved of God - The journey towards the pleasure of a changed mindset,

Where your renewed mind shall fully serve the love that is in your heart.

Be present/future with Me. I will teach you how to reorder your present thinking to include your future identity.

The emerging you has more favor, more power, more anointing, and more of My Presence.

I love who you are now, **and** I love the you that is emerging.

I will teach you to love both and to live in both.

I will show you how to bring the future into today, so that you will be free of the past and able to discover the person I have made you in Christ.

Perception is the key to power.
How you see yourself in Me will provide you
with the keys to victory in every situation.

See, I have already made you a warrior in the Spirit.
Everything is available to you.
You must learn to step into the reality of what I have
already made available in Jesus.

Let that identity settle into your heart.
It is My doing. By My permission do you enter My
provision.
Not by your performance.
Your performance is never about entering, it is about
ABIDING!!

Dear Heart, please get this!
You are already in Christ. I have placed you there.
You need not work to enter this high place.
It is your inheritance, freely given.

Beloved, you must work to remain there.
Your performance is not about earning, it is first
about ACCEPTING who you are to Me.
You must accept My heart towards you,
Become fully engaged in My great love for you.

Assignment

❅ Now that you are learning to be brilliant…let's see what you've got!

❅ Write your own assignment, and then do it.

Commission

❅ In this life God is giving you, what authority and power would you like to move in that would cause others to receive a breakthrough?

Personal Notes

Part 8....Be Thrilled with Your Tutor

I will teach you the lessons of beauty.
It is a great life I have given you.
I will teach you how to abide in Me,
The joy of dwelling in Me,
The beauty of just ... being in Me and with Me.

You must simply accept the upgrade of anointing that
I willingly bestow.
Learn sensitivity with the Holy Spirit.

The key to learning is to be thrilled by your tutor.
Let the enthusiasm of the Holy Spirit fill you up.
He loves to increase you!
He loves to show you who you are going to become
next.
He loves to declare the fullness of Jesus to you.

He has all your upgrades in His heart.
That is why He is permanently and perpetually
excited about your life and your identity.
He adores His role in your life.
He happily goes about the business each day of
developing a mindset in you that releases your
identity at the next level.
He loves to show you your destiny, then move you
towards it.

The key to your development and the speed of your growth …

is for you to become as enthusiastic about your identity as I AM.

I love who you are now, and I love the you that is coming.

I love the you that is being transformed,

And I love the you that is emerging **because** of the transformation.

Assignment

- ❄ Ask the Father to give you a revelation of the personality of the Holy Spirit.
- ❄ Compare and contrast what you receive with what you have been taught. What is the difference, and how will it affect the way you relate to the Holy Spirit?

Commission

- ❄ How will you minister to other people out of the personality, nature, and gifting of the Holy Spirit?

Personal Notes

Part 9....Becoming Warrior Class

A warrior spirit is My gift to you.
A warrior mindset is your gift to Me.
A warrior lifestyle is our partnership ... together.

Allow My Spirit ... Who is your helper ...
to forge a renewed mind in you ... that is Warrior
class.

A warrior mindset is always focused on victory.
It allows no possibility of defeat. It does not retreat.
It stands under extreme pressure.
It advances by My permission.

I, too, have a language of intimidation.
It's called worship. Your intimacy intimidates the
enemy.
Never forget ... that he is afraid of rejoicing hearts.
He cannot stay in the Presence of real praise.

You already have the victory.
Abiding is the key to experiencing it.
A mind set on Abiding cannot be overcome.

A warrior persona lives in joy and loves to rejoice!
It is fully immersed in a Spirit of Thanksgiving.
Rejoicing leads you into the place of being fully
occupied with Me.

Stand, be unmoved … it unnerves the enemy.
Do everything from rest.
Live a life supremely, unconcerned by the darkness.
Live a life that loves the light.

I will teach you about the power that comes from endurance.
I will show you the Supremacy that manifests itself in Patience.
Patience is a weapon of mass demoralization to the enemy.

He has no patience. His own impatience will defeat him.
Wait patiently by being active in worship.
Wait patiently and love the simplicity of prayer.
It's time for a new conversation.

The joy of My Presence will release more into the situation than the enemy can handle.
The object of warfare is victory. The objective of victory is Occupation.
First … be occupied with me.

I am seeking more than victory.
I seek territory.
I will teach you to reclaim your inner territory.
Then I will show you the particular piece of land in
the Spirit that I wish to give you.

I will teach you how to take it and how to hold it in
your identity in Me.

You are the hope of the nations,
A warrior class that changes the history of people
groups.
I have opened the door to a whole new dimension of
the Spirit,
To give you a taste of the power of the age to come.

To bring heaven to earth in My Name -
That is My purpose. On earth, as it is in heaven.
You must live from heaven to earth if you are to fully
glorify Me.

I have opened the door to a secret place in the Spirit.
It is My heart that you should fully explore this place
and discover who you really are in the process.
Then I will put this door in you so that My heart in
and for you,
Will open the door for others.
This is the year of your rising, Beloved.
Enter into a higher place in the Spirit.

It's time!

Assignment

❋ You are developing a warrior mindset. How
does your present thinking need to adjust and
be renewed for that mindset to be established?

❋ How can your intimacy intimidate the
enemy? What upgrade in worship is currently
available to you?

❋ Explain how Thanksgiving and Rejoicing will
affect the enemy as he tries to engage with
your life.

Commission

❋ What are your weapons of mass
demoralization, and how will you use them
against the enemy?

❋ Explain the power of patience and how it
combines with faith to cause you to inherit
the promise? Hebrews 6:12.

❋ What inner territory have you reclaimed, and
what values and principles have you learned
in the process?

Personal Notes

Other Books by Graham Cooke

❊ A Divine Confrontation… Birth Pangs of the New Church

❊ Developing Your Prophetic Gifting (Outdated and out of print. It is being replaced by The Prophetic Equipping Series Volumes 1-6.)

❊ The Prophetic Equipping Series, Volume 1 - Approaching the Heart of Prophecy.

❊ The Prophetic Equipping Series, Volume 2 - Prophecy & Responsibility

❊ The Prophetic Equipping Series, Volume 3 – Prophetic Wisdom

❊ The Being With God Series – The Nature of God, Hiddenness & Manifestation, Crafted Prayer, Beholding & Becoming, Towards A Powerful Inner Life, The Language Of Promise, God's Keeping Power and Living In Dependency & Wonder.

❊ Way of the Warrior Series, Volume 1-3 Qualities of a Spiritual Warrior , Manifesting Your Spirit and Coming Into Alignment

❊ The Wisdom Series, Secret Sayings Hidden Meanings

Co-author:

❊ Permission Granted with Gary Goodell

Welcome to
Brilliant
BOOK HOUSE

Reaching Christians For Christ

G raham Cooke is an acclaimed writer who started writing twenty years ago, releasing his first in 1990 which sold cover 400,000 copies worldwide. Graham has since rewritten this material into a new edition called The Prophetic Equipping Series, which will be six volumes. Volumes 1-3 are available now, Approaching the Heart of Prophecy, Prophecy & Responsibility and Prophetic Wisdom.

Download Graham's e-books today!

All of Graham's books and interactive journals are available to download directly onto your computer, eliminating shipping costs!

Graham has written over 14 titles, on subjecting ranging from how to craft a prayer, understanding what is really going on in the spirit when God seems to be distant and when He is drawing close, understanding God's nature and many many others.

Brilliant boasts an extensive collection of Graham's work. We distribute his CDs, MP3s, DVDs, Books and Interactive Journals and offer a direct link between graham and our customers through our newsletters, YouTube channel and podcasts.

" **A**t Brilliant Book House, we believe you have a unique call on your life that can only be found in God. He has something for you that is far beyond your wildest dreams. As you step out into that purpose, we want to stand with you, offering you encouragement, training, and hope for your journey. We want to equip you for what God wants to do in you, and through you. That is our promise to you. "

Graham Cooke

Brilliant Book House is a California-based publishing company founded and directed by Graham Cooke and is dedicated to producing high-quality Christian resources and teaching materials. Our vision is to equip all of our readers to lead brilliant lives, confidently led by the Holy Spirit into the destiny God has for you.

Brilliant has a passion for the Kingdom of Heaven; a powerful desire to see the Body of Christ comes into full dynamic stature in the earth; and a hunger for everyone in Jesus to discover their rightful place in the purposes of God.

The world needs to see God in a *brilliant* way.

Visit us online today:

www.BrilliantBookHouse.com